H. Stephen Glenn, Ph.D., and Jane Nelsen, Ed.D.

Raising Self-Reliant Children in a Self-Indulgent World

REVISED EDITION

Seven Building Blocks for Developing Capable Young People

 THREE RIVERS PRESS · NEW YORK

Published by Three Rivers Press, New York, New York.
Member of the Crown Publishing Group, a division of Random House, Inc.
www.randomhouse.com

THREE RIVERS PRESS and the Tugboat design are registered trademarks of Random House, Inc.

Originally published by Prima Publishing, Roseville, California, in 2000.

Illustrations by Paula Gray

40 Developmental Assets reprinted with permission from The Search Institute, *Developmental Assets Among Minneapolis Youth* (Minneapolis, MN: Search Institute, 1996). All rights reserved by Search Institute, 1-800-888-7828. Search Institute, 2000.

Printed in the United States of America

Library of Congress Cataloging-in-Publication Data
Glenn, H. Stephen.
    Raising self-reliant children in a self-indulgent world : seven building blocks for developing capable young people / H. Stephen Glenn, Jane Nelsen.
        p. cm.
    Includes bibliographical references and index.
1. Child Rearing. 2. Child development. 3. Self-reliance in children. 4. Success. I. Nelsen, Jane. II. Title.
HQ769 .G645 2000
649'.1—dc21   00-040660

ISBN 0-7615-1128-8

10 9 8 7 6

First Edition

*"In times of change, learners inherit the earth,
while the learned find themselves beautifully equipped
to deal with a world that no longer exists."*
—Eric Hoffer

. . .

To Learners Everywhere

CONTENTS

ACKNOWLEDGMENTS

Our understanding of this topic has been greatly heightened and enhanced by thousands of people over the last twenty years who have shared with us their personal struggles and their personal successes in the hope that they would increase people's understanding of families in our changing world.

I, Stephen Glenn, would like first to acknowledge my parents, Harold and Helen Glenn, whose more than sixty years of marriage have provided a great model. Next, I would like to thank my four children, Keri Marie, Kristi Lyn, Kimbi Lee, and Michael who have raised a fairly capable father and have been willing to help me go through the trial and error process in learning to be one.

I would also like to acknowledge Dale and Rita Miller, who have spent nearly sixty years together raising my wife Judy Arleen. And to Judy—she has brought me Jennifer, John and Becky to help raise and is sharing the experience of our twelve grandchildren with me.

Finally, I would like to acknowledge Jane Nelsen, who challenged me to sit down and record the many thoughts and ideas spoken in my workshops and speeches over the years. Without her discipline this book might never have been written.

I, Jane Nelsen, would like to acknowledge the inspiration Stephen has been in my life as in so many others' lives. The principles presented in this book have been extremely helpful in our family. It is a privilege to be instrumental in making this material available in book form.

Special appreciation goes to Barry, Mark, and Mary for their patience, support, and self-reliance during this project and in general. They are extremely capable people.

We deeply appreciate our Prima editors, Shawn Vreeland and Jamie Miller, for their patience and encouragement—and Paula Gray for making the book more fun to read with her fabulous illustrations.

INTRODUCTION

The Challenge That Faces Us

THE PROCESS OF GROWING from weak to strong, from dependent to independent, from incapable to capable is called *habilitation*.

Steve spent eight years in higher education studying rehabilitation, and never in all those years was the concept of habilitation discussed. It was his young daughter who really challenged him with the idea. She was learning about dictionaries and wanted to help him with a paper he was working on, so he asked her to look up *rehabilitation*. The definition she found was "to restore to former excellence."

Steve began to laugh. His daughter asked, "What's so funny, Dad?"

He replied, "I was just thinking about all my clients. It's hard for me to believe that every struggling adolescent was once an excellent individual who forgot how to be excellent, or that every struggling alcoholic was once an excellent recovering alcoholic and gave it up for some unknown reason. I can't believe that every chronically inadequate family was once an excellent family that lost sight of its goals. It is my impression that virtually all the people I've served in my career have been struggling to attain something that had never been within reach for them before."

She said, "Well, Dad, didn't you always tell me that when you look up a word with *re-* in front of it that it's very helpful to look up the word without the *re-* to see what it is you are redoing?"

"Yes, that's what I usually do."

"Well, then," she said, "we should look up *habilitation*."

They couldn't find the word habilitation in their *Webster's Dictionary* at home, so they went to the library to search the larger dictionary there. "It's here!" she cried in excitement when they came upon the word.

The definition given for *habilitation* was "to clothe." That didn't ring a bell, so they looked up the reference that was given, which led them to a chart showing the evolution of the human race. On the chart was a series of figures beginning with apes moving along to increasingly upright primates and ending with a man in a three-piece suit with a briefcase. The first figures were naked and hairy, but in the middle of the chart one was dressed in fur "jogging shorts." After that, the figures were fully clothed. The first fully clothed figure was labeled *Homo habilus,* translated as "man the able" or "the capable." From the root word *habilus* we get "ability" or "capability." The first alleged progenitor of the human race who acquired capabilities to act on the environment rather than react to it was called "human the able or capable." *Capabilities distinguished humans from animals.*

With this definition in hand, Steve's daughter, with marvelous childlike logic, said, "Then aren't you trying to do something that was never done in the first place?"

Steve said with a smile, "Where were you about $30 billion worth of federal programs ago with that kind of logic and insight?" He was referring to the many organizations and institutions that for years have tried to rehabilitate— "to restore to former excellence"—people who were never habilitated in the first place.

Most people in rehabilitation programs have never been capable, productive, or independent. In reality, they do not need rehabilitation. They need habilitation.

Human beings arrive in this world without capabilities and have to acquire them in an apprenticeship. *Webster's* helps again here by defining apprentice as "one who is learning by practical experience under skilled workers."

The last half of the twentieth century saw massive changes in American Society, many of which undercut the ability of many families to provide opportunities for young people to engage in an apprenticeship of habilitation to prepare them for life. For our forebears, most of whom lived in rural environments, life proceeded at a relatively slow pace. They had time to adapt to external changes. But today we are caught in a vortex of technological and societal change that is whirling ever faster. Instead of the stability and familiarity our grandparents knew, we are faced with the need to adapt to constantly changing conditions. Americans, like people of many other nations, are crossing a frontier of knowledge and technology expanding at a rate unprecedented in history. Nowhere is the stress of that journey more evident than among families and young people.

Declining Achievement, Motivation, and Discipline

THE STEADILY EMERGING BASE of statistical evidence in the United States indicates that beginning with the children born in 1946, the baby boomers who became the class of '63, achievement began a steady downward trend that persisted over the next twenty years. That wonderful flock of post-war children, born to high hopes in 1946, struggled to reach their potential. They took the achievement tests in 1963 and became the first group of children in one hundred years to move significantly *downward* instead of *upward* in their scores. Their problems did not end with low academic scores. They also set records in the areas that are plaguing our youth today: crime and vandalism, teenage pregnancy, drug and alcohol abuse, and suicide.

Records in all these areas continued to be broken by each class for twenty years. From 1963 to 1983, every succeeding graduating class scored lower in achievement, motivation, and discipline than the class before, and they showed marked increases in the destructive behaviors.

What was going on? In retrospect, we can see that the class of 1963 formed a vanguard—a generation of children born to a brand-new lifestyle. This lifestyle reflected a drastic population shift from a primarily rural and small-town setting to an urban/suburban environment. It brought enticing technological innovations—radio, television, electronics, computers, lasers—that by themselves seemed to offer remarkable opportunities. But the increase in leisure and the decrease in family/community interdependence began to weaken the traditional support systems that served to habilitate our young people.

We cannot turn back the clock, nor would we want to, but we can re-create opportunities that helped produce healthy youth in the past. Indeed, it *is* possible to combine the best of past and present lifestyles. In this book we will examine how to do that successfully.

An Historical Overview

A CAREFUL LOOK BACKWARD will help us identify the major differences between the past and the present and how they relate to the critical areas of need within our families.

For centuries, children were raised in the lifestyle and traditions of their parents. They adapted to those traditions and developed the basic capabilities to function effectively within those lifestyles. The result was relative stability within families.

At the end of World War II, however, thousands of families moved away from networks of grandmothers, grandfathers, aunts, uncles, cousins, nieces, and nephews. They left their small towns, villages, and farms, which had been the basis for family life, and found themselves in larger urban and suburban settings. Often unable to find stable niches, they kept moving. By 1986, the average family was moving every four and a half years and knew very little about their current neighbors and community.

In the smaller, more stable rural settings, children were offered opportunities to learn life skills through on-the-job training because they were needed to help the family function and survive. On the other hand, in the new urban/suburban settings, children did not have real opportunities to learn the skills they needed to become capable adults. They were not needed in the day-to-day functioning of families. They frequently spent a large portion of their time watching television, which included a variety of programs and concepts that were counterproductive to the development of skills and capabilities necessary for successful living.

Today, increasing numbers of children have fewer and fewer opportunities to experience a meaningful role in family life and social institutions. *Without a meaningful role, it is difficult to develop a sense of meaning, purpose, and significance through being needed, listened to, and taken seriously.*

The struggle to raise capable children has become more difficult for families who have not learned to compensate for the things that were lost in the rapid lifestyle changes. Capabilities that were once acquired so naturally in the old circumstances have now weakened. And that lack of strength in skills and capabilities threatens the potential of our young people today.

Stressful Relationships

RELATIONSHIPS BETWEEN SPOUSES HAVE become more tenuous and stressful. Our culture is experiencing a rapid increase in reported incidents of spouse abuse, child abuse, desertion, neglect, and sedative and alcohol dependency. In part, this surge of problems is reflected by increased statistical aware-ness. (In other words, we are finally willing to acknowledge that these problems exist.) However, whenever appropriate allowances have been made for in-creased awareness, significant increases in the actual incidence of these prob-lems have occurred.

Overall, we can say that the stable underpinning of family relationships has gradually weakened. And in a corollary trend, stability in schools, jobs, and community support systems has also been undermined.

The Fading of the Great American Dream

THESE TROUBLING SYMPTOMS CONTINUED to escalate, and by the 1970s, it became almost a platitude to suggest that the great American dream was faltering. We became confused in our attempt to explain what was happen-ing. Because the sixties were so turbulent, we looked to that decade for answers.

Some theorists suggested that we were the terminal victims of urbaniza-tion, technology, future shock, and the nuclear age. Conservatives suggested that we were the victims of divorce, working mothers, and single-parent fami-lies and that as long as we allowed these conditions to persist, we would have to accept our struggle as normal.

Some of what we called the sixties dropouts were happy to support these theories. If it was suggested to them that perhaps the reason they did not want to apply themselves was due to the nuclear age, they would readily agree. They would not admit that they simply preferred to sit around and get "high" be-cause they had not learned through practice the relevance of self-discipline and hard work.

Once we came to our senses and began to look more thoughtfully at the situation, we clearly could not hold any single factor accountable for produc-ing the conditions with which we were dealing.

Hopeful Outlook

TO SUGGEST THAT ONE FACTOR is responsible is much like saying one snowflake causes an avalanche or that one grain of sand tips the balance on a scale. So we began to look for contributing factors. In taking a longer view, we saw the sixties as a product of the thirties, forties, and fifties. That is, we observed that a continuum, not a sudden disruption, accounted for our social difficulties.

It is now apparent that the problem was not rooted simply in technology and urbanization per se but in our lack of understanding as to how to compensate for the changes these phenomena brought about. This perspective offers a far more hopeful outlook and a wealth of options.

At the same time, we began to look more carefully at children who were thriving in spite of urbanization, rapid technological change, single-parent status, divorce, poverty, affluence, and future shock. Their example also yielded a new and more hopeful perspective.

Breakthroughs

AS WE THOUGHTFULLY COMPARE successful individuals with individuals who are average or below average in their struggles and productivity, we begin to achieve many breakthroughs in our understanding. We are finding models that all of us can use. Studying the lives of unusually successful families and individuals in today's world points the way toward a more successful future.

We *can* avoid the downward trends in achievement and self-discipline and the upward trends in crime and vandalism, teenage pregnancy, drug and alcohol abuse, and teenage suicide.

Slow Acceptance of New Knowledge

FORTUNATELY, THE WHOLE FIELD of family and human relations is benefiting from the current explosion of knowledge and technology. The information we are reaping is exciting. However, the acceptance of new knowledge usually occurs very slowly. For example, there was a time when one out of every four women who gave birth to a baby died from a disease called childbirth fever. We now know the deaths were caused by infections from bacteria introduced by the physician's unclean hands. Dr. Ignaz Semmelweis discovered that by washing his hands he could reduce the mortality rate of his patients to only 8 percent. He tried to spread this wonderful knowledge but was considered a quack by his colleagues. It took more than one hundred years before the medical community was convinced of the validity of this discovery and all doctors began washing their hands. We can only hope our new knowledge about families will generally be accepted and put to use more quickly. It seems this hope is not misplaced.

Fathers Joining the Team: A Positive Factor

WE HAVE BEEN PRESENTING PROGRAMS on "Raising Capable Young People and Positive Discipline" for many years. Several years ago the vast majority of our participants were female. It was obvious that the culture still considered child rearing as "woman's work." But something wonderful has begun to happen. Over the last few years more and more fathers have begun participating. And today nearly one-third of our participants, in both our daytime and evening programs, are fathers. Apparently, these men decided parenting is a collaborative project involving both parents.

A few years ago, in a little town outside Indianapolis, we were conducting a community awareness series. As part of this series we held an evening on "Fathering for Fathers." Ten fathers showed up—nine of them married to the committee members who planned the evening and one who got stuck in his driveway without an alibi and was dragged to the occasion. By contrast, we recently held another series in that same community, and 390 fathers came, causing a standing-room-only crowd. And these men came despite the fact that the school held a sports appreciation banquet at the same time.

To their credit, more than several fathers organized, went to the banquet, paid for their spaghetti, shook hands with the coaches, and then announced, "The best thing we can do to support this program is to get our act together as fathers. Any of you who agree, come with us." One hundred ninety of those fathers left the banquet and came to the session on fathering. This action represents an increasingly hopeful and persistent trend because it illustrates that the interest in conquering family problems is emanating from inside the family itself. It is this element—strong motivation on the part of parents—that is critical to the kinds of problem solving we endorse.

Baby Boomers as Fathers

IT IS INTERESTING TO NOTE that our new solutions may be emerging from the heart of the problem. After the troubled sixties, there was much speculation on how baby boomers would fare as parents after going through so much turmoil and self-indulgence. A recent *Time/Life* survey indicated that baby boomer fathers are spending four to five times the amount of personal time educating two children than their fathers devoted to five children.

This increase in father participation might explain why in the recent past and present a significant number of young people are becoming more achievement oriented and are exhibiting more admiration for their parents. Two-thirds of all American young people recently surveyed indicated that they had substantial admiration for their parents and considered them among their heroes. We believe that the increased interest in active parenting by fathers helps in gaining their children's respect. Moreover, it is also helping address another significant issue: the absence of working mothers from the home for significant periods of time.

A Turning Point

EACH YEAR WE STUDY the National Senior Survey, a detailed study of the attitudes of high school graduates. In 1978 and 1979, this survey indicated that the percentage of young people who had a strong future orientation, clear goals, and assertiveness about personal beliefs was at an all-time low. The survey showed that the decline in those characteristics had coincided with an increase in marijuana use among young people. However, recent National Senior Surveys (1983 through 1995) showed a reversal of these trends. Significantly more seniors were involved in such activities as student government, community service, and goal orientation toward the future. Simultaneously, marijuana use declined among young people. These classes also did better on the achievement tests than classes from previous years. It is sobering to observe that in the 1996 National Senior Survey some of these upward trends appeared to be stagnating, at least temporarily. We cannot rest on slight gains. Still, we can allow ourselves some optimism in the face of the recent surveys.

Limited Only by Our Ability to Dream

IT HAS BEEN SAID THAT *a nation that does not stand firmly for something will ultimately stand for anything.* The turbulence of the sixties and seventies presented a number of problems for our communities and our families that caused us to lose sight of the principles that made the United States strong. Now, however, we are showing signs of once again developing a vision of who we are, where we can go, and what we can accomplish. When we share such a vision with our children, we inspire them to work toward these ends. The Great American Dream does not need to die. Right now it is like a garden suffering from a lack of cultivation.

Need for Learners

PERHAPS THE CHALLENGE WE face as the rearers and educators of young people is stated best by Eric Hoffer: "In times of change, learners inherit the earth, while the learned find themselves beautifully equipped to deal with a world that no longer exists."

A theologian recently pointed out that a similar injunction was offered by Christ in the New Testament when he said, "Blessed are the meek, for they shall inherit the earth." The meek in that context did not mean weak, down-looking individuals but rather those humble enough to be teachable.

In whatever form we find it, this counsel is important for us today. We face challenges unprecedented in history. We cannot be arrogant enough to say, "Well, that is the way my parents did it" or "Our family always handled it that way." We must ponder thoughtfully and ask, "What was it we were accomplishing in our family by doing it that way?" and "What ways do we have today to accomplish that same thing?"

Splitting the wood and walking to the cowshed gave us the physical activity necessary for our bodies to maintain health as well as to get needed chores done. Today we may need to compensate and participate in recreational walking, aerobics, or a workout center to accomplish the same benefits.

In this same sense, we can compensate for the rapid changes of our society by thoughtfully learning how to prepare our young people to have the tools, the capabilities, and the beliefs of the learner. Much of this book will offer ways to accomplish this.

Must Be Learners Rather than Learned

IN THIS BOOK, WE want to encourage the reader to use every available means to explore ways to make the family thrive. This is not an easy task. Society applauds those who pursue an education to prepare for a career. However, it has not yet adequately acknowledged the value of vigorous exploration in the area of family and personal relationships. But this should not deter us. Like the pioneers who huddled together around campfires to share resources and information, we need to ask friends and neighbors for information, read books, attend classes, talk openly about the struggles and dilemmas we face—and always remain thoughtful about the information we collect. We can then use our own wisdom to apply the knowledge we gain to our unique life situation.

The point here is that we all must be information gatherers and must teach our children how to find knowledge themselves. Human knowledge in our culture is expanding at the rate of 100 percent every five years. In some fields a 100 percent gain in new knowledge every eleven months is not unusual. Many futurists project that if these trends continue, this year's first graders will have to be equipped on graduation day to handle a 100 percent knowledge explosion every thirty-eight days. This means that the information in every book they read the first of the month will have to be updated by the end of the month. And that's why we agree with Eric Hoffer that in such a world it is as important for our children to be given the generic tools of the learner as it is to integrate the accumulated data of the past. To ensure that we do this is a great challenge indeed, for both educators and parents.

Tools of the Learner

IN STUDYING THE CHARACTERISTICS of learners, we have identified a number of critical concepts, capabilities, and beliefs that we will refer to in this book as the *Significant Seven*. The Significant Seven comprise three beliefs or

perceptions of the world and four skills that are the essence of fully functioning human beings. Helping young people develop these perceptions and skills
adequately will necessitate specific changes in the practices of many parents
and teachers. And it will require that we significantly change the experience
base of many young people to allow them opportunities to develop the necessary perceptions and skills for successful living.

Our Focus

IN THE FOLLOWING CHAPTERS, we provide blueprints for the strategies
and activities through which parents, teachers, and other adults can encourage
young people to develop the significant perceptions and skills. It is our hope
that through this process we can give encouragement and direction to the efforts of parents, teachers, families, and, most important, young people, in realizing their own potential.

Families in Transition

IN THE 1930S, most children were enthusiastic about finding ways to improve their lot in life. Because life was hard, they grew up fast and had to become self-reliant. Because they were needed and considered important assets, they usually made significant contributions to their family's well-being.

Respect for, and obedience to, elders was the expected standard. So the thought of behaving otherwise was seldom entertained. Parents didn't consider parenting classes because they rarely encountered behavior problems, and they usually didn't have the luxury of trying to prepare their children with the kind of life skills that would prepare them for a "better" life. Education (which was seen as a life-changing opportunity) frequently took a backseat to the needs of the family economy. When they could go to school, their work generally reflected the positive qualities their parents had imbued in them: self-discipline, responsibility, good judgment, and perseverance.

After World War II, life changed drastically. America's growing affluence began to encourage self-indulgence. By the 1960s, a growing number of children, who no longer felt needed as contributors and had little encouragement to be self-reliant, began to lose direction in their preparation for life. (They had not had to put forth much effort to contribute and cooperate in the family. Why start now?)

As a result, many also lost interest in bettering their circumstances (since they were already doing well by world standards). Too often, school became irrelevant and therefore boring. Heroes and models in society promised immediate gratification through television, drugs, alcohol, and sex. Many young people became sullen and disrespectful to their elders, since the norms and morals of society were now unclear. Schoolwork, for many, began to reflect their declining motivation and capabilities.

By many standards, the world is a much better place today than it was forty years ago. Still, in the past, we could assume that children growing up, if they survived physically, would be equipped with the capabilities to act in their own behalf and pursue opportunities as adults (though far fewer opportunities were available).

Today, when the world offers far more and greater opportunities for achievement and success than ever before (for those who have the capabilities and motivation), the rising generation seems less capable than the generation of the thirties to take advantage of the opportunities open to them. It is clear that some of the fundamental values that served us so well in the past are absent or severely underdeveloped in a large percentage of young people. Let's take a look at those values.

> The challenge today is to help children develop the self-reliance, commitment, and skills that were the standard thirty to fifty years ago.

For centuries, people worried about finding opportunities for themselves and ways to ensure that their children would have more than they did. Many of our ancestors, motivated by the possibility of greater opportunity in America, decided to break old ties, leave their homelands, and sail to America in the holds of crowded ships. They took this chance knowing the risk: one-third of the people died before reaching the promised shore. They hoped to be lucky enough to survive and find room in the New World—a piece of land to own—unlike their families, who had been tenants for centuries.

Some risked their lives for the dream of owning a business and the distant possibility of growing rich, so that they could give their children advantages they themselves had never had. They came to America, faced an alien environment, and claimed a share of the world's largest, richest, and most vital country. They did this with self-reliance, initiative, courage, and resourcefulness. Knowing the price that had been paid, the second generation usually continued working hard to improve the land or business their parents had worked and sometimes died for. In so doing, they continued to model the qualities they had acquired from their parents. However, by trying to save their children from the hardships they had endured, they often indulged their children. They did not realize that their hardships helped them build courage, character, and strength and that by giving their children too much with too little effort on their part, their children did not have the opportunity to build the same qualities.

Today, by comparison, children often seem critically deficient in resources for effective living. Since they live in a world of unprecedented possibilities for resourceful, self-reliant people, the challenge today is to help children develop the self-reliance, motivation, and skills that were the standard thirty to fifty years ago.

To some extent, the once-prevailing expectation that young people would take on the same roles as their parents was oppressive. Nevertheless, by fulfilling it, children served a valuable apprenticeship. By the time they had reached adolescence, they were under very few illusions about the meaning of crop failures (or other economic crises), the time and effort it took to get from place to place, or the amount of time it took their family to save up for new shoes or something special for Christmas.

Still, within this reality, life held many mysteries for adolescents. What was romance all about? What happened once you got married? Few children had any real awareness of what adults talked about when they were together privately. The world of children consisted largely of interactions with siblings, cousins, friends, and classmates (children of all ages rather than age-mates in a single peer group). In short, childhood in those days was an internship for life. There were many resources to encourage the growth of self-discipline, good judgment, and responsibility, but there were limitations, too. Technology was primitive, and travel required time and patience. It was difficult to communicate with people who lived far away. And there were very few jobs and career opportunities. Most young people could only hope to follow in their parents' footsteps: work the family farm, grow up in the family business, or, if the family was poor, struggle for survival and hope for a lucky break.

For many, the chance for an education was a rare thing; it was common to start working early in life, dropping out of school to do so. Even becoming literate was a distant dream for most people. Then, in what amounted to a quantum leap at the end of World War II, everything changed. In two decades, opportunities began exploding, travel became easy, and communication became efficient.

However, as discussed in the introduction, the cost of these developments was a dismantling of most of our basic training mechanisms for young people.

Today we find that far too many American children at the onset of puberty face an incredible "smorgasbord" of opportunities with a deficiency in capabilities. Self-confidence, self-validation, self-discipline, good judgment, and a sense of responsibility are all lacking, and our children find themselves incapable of carving out assets for themselves and ill equipped to take advantage of the opportunities.

Consider the irony. Today's children will be *forced* to accept more years of education than most people in history could even dream of having. And to many of our young people today, education seems like a curse.

In decades past, children who had to split cords of firewood, chase runaway animals, or walk behind the mule for hours plowing sometimes viewed school as a wonderful alternative, a luxurious life of leisure. Today, however, what is the alternative to attending school? The answer, in part, is eating snack foods, throwing Frisbees, watching rock videos and soap operas, wandering around town, smoking a little dope, drinking a few six-packs, zoning out in front of the TV. What's the logical choice for someone seeking an easy time of it? More industrious children spend hours surfing the Internet or learning "hacking" skills far beyond what they could learn in school.

Our job on behalf of our children today is to equip them with the capabilities that no longer accrue automatically from daily life. It's a challenge but a thrilling one, for it is far better to be standing seminaked before a great array of possibilities than to be clothed for a journey but frustrated by the lack of opportunity.

PASSING VALUES

HOW DO WE MEET THE challenge? By taking lessons from the past. There was a time in America when the attitudes, values, and behavior of each generation were effectively passed on to the next generation through interaction between the generations. Teenage boys and girls could step in and fill the roles of their parents if they needed to.

In the rural, small-town environment, children often worked ten hours a day alongside one or both parents. They received on-the-job training as they watched their parents doing essential work, making decisions, and discussing values. Very early, children became participants rather than mere observers in the adult, work-a-day world. In the evenings after the work was done, children participated in mealtime discussions, learned handicrafts, and made clothing and other things actually used in the home or for work. Brothers and sisters, parents and children, grandparents and other relatives worked together, played together, and often learned to read and write from each other.

This extended-family network usually provided a nurturing environment for children. If a father disciplined his son too heavily, Grandma was often there to soothe and say, "He was like that when he was a boy, too, but you had better go along and do what he says." In this way, even the strictest, most authoritarian discipline could be moderated, given positive meaning and thus made more acceptable.

Equally effective were the lessons that life itself taught through the consequences that stemmed from real-life actions. If the child assigned to do the milking forgot to milk the cow for three days, the family went without milk until the cow had another calf. If the children did not pull the weeds, in three months there would be no vegetables to eat. Even the three-year-olds learned "what happens if. . . ." When they failed to gather eggs, there would be none for breakfast. Thus, many children grew up with capabilities because much of their experience had significance, meaning, purpose, and relevance to their daily lives. Because these children were often needed, they were also respected and taken seriously, thus experiencing the positive consequences of doing their work well.

In this context, school did not bear the burden of education alone. Rural people had very limited access to information. Parents formed groups, pooled resources, and hired teachers whose values and behavior were in harmony with their own. The home and school worked in partnership, to prepare individuals for successful living. In this lifestyle, raising capable young people was a natural result of a collaboration between family and community.

Compare these scenes with what often happens in too many homes today. Everyone is too busy going in too many different directions, doing too many things. When they are home, each family member is often isolated in a different room with his or her own TV. Children may know the name of their parents' (both of them) jobs but have no idea what they actually do. A recent study conducted by Hawkins and Catalano showed that many children are becoming sexually active or involved in gangs before they become teenagers because their families are "disconnected." Parents are too busy to give their children time, so they give them things, such as their own TVs, cars, designer clothes, and a large allowance to spend on CDs, movies, and junk foods. (Another study showed that the average weekly allowance for teens is $50— a shocking amount to many adults who had difficulty talking their parents into $20 a month.) What happened to cause such drastic changes?

THE URBAN REVOLUTION

IN 1930, ACCORDING TO THE census, 70 percent of all Americans lived on farms or in small communities. By 1950, a complete reversal had occurred: Nearly 70 percent lived in an urban/suburban environment, and only one-third lived on farms or in small communities. And even those in a rural environment had an urban lifestyle. They commuted to work, had television in their homes, and had their children bused to school.

As a result of this radical change, the integrity of relationships diminished all the way around. Families moved from living rooms filled with dialogue to family rooms dominated by electronic devices. As a result, conversation became unlikely. Once we had kitchens filled with rituals, traditions, and collaboration, and supper table conversation extending until bedtime. This was frequently the most affirming and attractive activity available.

Now we have rooms full of machines that pour noise and images into our homes and wipe out all personal interactions. We traded our wagons, which moved so slowly that we had no alternative but to talk to one another, for metal cylinders that race down freeways while cassette tape players and FM radios absorb our attention. It is now possible to travel all the way across the country and never have to say more than, "Are you sure you have to go now?"

Other losses were never compensated for by even an undesirable substitute. In 1940, at least one grandparent was a full-time, active member of approximately 60 to 70 percent of all households. Today, fewer than 2 percent of our families have a grandparent available as a resource. In 1940, a full-time homemaker spent approximately thirty-nine hours a week on domestic chores in more than 90 percent of all households. Today, close to 80 percent of all children who return home from school in America enter a household in which every living member has been gone for the best ten hours of the day. Once the family assembles, all the routine business of the household is still to be done. It takes an average of thirty-seven hours a week to accomplish the domestic chores, but in most households there is no one around all day to do them. The need to get chores done after a long day at work competes with any remaining time for high-quality interaction. By the time we scurry around putting food on the table, washing and sorting clothes, taking care of other chores, issuing warnings, perhaps spending a moment in the tub, the day is over. If we are not careful, we sacrifice two things we cannot afford to lose: the dialogue and collaboration that affirms our sense of ourselves.

What is the essence of the problem? Though we have cited urban immigration as transitional, large communities are not the problem in themselves. The European migrants who moved to large cities in the United States prior to World War II stayed together in small districts with relatives and friends where they continued to live in much the same way as they had in their native countries. These people attended religious institutions together, held the same festivals, maintained the old traditions, and put their children in neighborhood schools in which the teachers were frequently people of their own ethnic backgrounds. In short, in the midst of the city, these people managed to create and maintain a small-town environment.

The Asian community in San Francisco is another example. It had an exemplary record in terms of stability and was notable for its lack of involvement with the criminal justice and social welfare systems—until the end of World War II. The community support systems then began to weaken, and many Asians became part of the amorphous, urban/suburban lifestyle.

Thus, urbanization per se was not the problem. Rather, it was the manner in which we made the rural/urban transition that wrenched our way of life. We left behind rituals, traditions, culture, social networks, and support systems and became isolated from one another.

Older readers will recall that in 1930 children spent three to four hours a day personally involved with various members of their extended families—parents, grandparents, aunts, uncles, and others who lived close by. Today's typical youngsters have a very different home experience. The extended family has been reduced to what we call the nuclear family—one or two parents plus the children. Relatives typically live far away.

> In less than thirty years, we have gone from a society with a surplus of significant communication among the generations, to a society in which that kind of significant interaction is the rare exception.

Interaction within nuclear families today amounts to only a few minutes a day. Of these few minutes, more than half are not true interaction. Rather, they are one-way communications delivered in a negative tone: parents' warnings or reproaches to children for misbehavior.

To summarize, the impact of our society's rapid social transition on the amount and quality of family interaction alone has been profound. Urbanization and the type of employment it created have virtually eliminated the likelihood that children will work *for any significant portion of a typical day* alongside one or both parents. This means that not only the amount but also the quality of parent-child interaction has been drastically reduced.

THE BIRTH OF TELEVISION

IN THE 1940S, A TECHNOLOGICAL innovation arrived that was destined to have a massive social impact. Though good can be said of television, this medium introduced into the average home attitudes, values, and behaviors completely foreign to most parents of the time. Of greatest significance is the fact that television quickly became the hub of social and leisure time in our society. In 1970, the average American watched television for five hours per day. It doesn't take a statistical genius to understand that those five hours of television viewing, when added to work time, commute time, sleep time, and personal hygiene, leave only about one hour for *potential* family interaction. And this doesn't count mealtimes and the normal business of the family. So, we used our ingenuity! We have discovered that mealtime and viewing time can be combined. Of course, this doubling up occurs at the expense of all the discussion and sharing that in pretelevision times was the norm at the dinner table. So when do families talk? If a family diligently uses forty-five minutes of the remaining hour every day for routine duties, *fifteen minutes are left over for meaningful interaction.*

In less than thirty years, then, we have gone from a society with a surplus of significant communication among the generations, to a society in which that kind of significant interaction is the rare exception.

HOSPITALS AND SCHOOLS IN CRISIS

WE HAVE SEEN SOME OF the insidious effects of urbanization on the family. Many of the underpinnings for children's development were disappearing.

Unfortunately, since this was not recognized, parents did not alter their behavior. One aspect of family life that remained unchanged during the same period had to do with the number of children in a family. An enormous number of couples who married after the war and who came from rural, small-town settings, where existing room and resources could support five or more children in a family, continued in the tradition of having five or more children. The newly urbanized couples often proceeded on the assumption that opportunities in the cities would bring advantages to their children, that they themselves might even become rich and be able to provide for the children as never before. In addition, the war itself, which had just ended, created a tremendous hunger in people to start new families. In this way—subtly—a crisis began in 1946. The first place it showed up was in the hospitals.

In 1946, the number of births in the urban/suburban setting was more than double that of the year before. Society was ill equipped to handle the onslaught of new arrivals. Hospitals were overtaxed, and a significant number of children were born in hallways, waiting rooms, or wherever makeshift facilities could be provided.

No one heeded the implications. These children lived for five years before it occurred to anyone that they would soon be going to school. On or around September 1, 1951, a mass of 4.2 million urban/suburban babies hit the schools looking for classrooms, teachers, and books. Taking everyone by surprise—for few people had heeded the warning embedded in the soaring 1946 birthrate—five times the number of children who had arrived the year before to start the first grade arrived at school and said, "Where is my seat?"

School people asked, "Where did you come from?"

Kids said, "We've been here for five years. We thought you saw us coming."

They hadn't. In an hour's time on that first day of school, those children forced a total change in the system. Almost overnight educators threw together what was later described as "a maladaptive response to a crisis situation" and called it public education. In the subsequent thirty years, data suggests that makeshift solutions worked for very few students and actually proved deleterious for most. They were also bad for teachers. On the students' side, a marked increase in the dropout rate and other forms of resistance to education took place. And among teachers hired into this new system, the tenure on the job decreased. By the early 1980s, the normal tenure was thirteen years.

Despite the years of preparation it took to become a teacher, the average educator was unhappy enough to switch careers midstream.

When teachers were asked why they were leaving, the most common response was "Everywhere I go in my profession there are too many people in the same place at the same time with too much to do and too little time to do it. I find it depressing to watch young people slip away for lack of the few minutes of attention and encouragement I never seem to be able to get around to giving them. I'm hoping that by changing careers now, perhaps to social work, real estate, or counseling, I can contribute to someone's life before my career is over."

School just wasn't working. Young people who needed more dialogue and collaboration, such as gifted children, or those who functioned better in listening and speaking than they did in reading and writing, or children with differences in learning rates and styles (we might call them learning disabled or just significantly unique human beings), began to show that they were not being stimulated by the school experience. The system was rife with stereotypical assumptions—for example, that all ten-year-olds would be ready for the same thing on the same day and could be tested and evaluated

There is a possible antidote to the steady diminishment of dialogue and collaboration at school. That is the increase at home of those activities necessary to encourage growth and learning in young people.

based on their responses. There was simply no provision for and no appreciation of individual differences.

In the bygone one-room schoolhouse, older children had served as teachers' aides and tutors for the younger ones. Not only was this of benefit to young students, it was also helpful to the older students. Tutoring had given older children a *meaningful role.* When the baby boom hit the urban/suburban schools, we grouped students by chronological age and sent all the natural tutors and teachers' aides to their own classrooms. Then we put as many as forty children into a single classroom with only one teacher and no teachers' aides. Needless to say, the time spent in classroom dialogue declined dramatically. With thirty to forty kids for fifty minutes, minus twenty minutes for required paperwork activities, only about forty seconds were left per class for each child to speak his or her mind—if that time was allotted equally. However, if, perish the thought, another child got excited and spoke for a couple of minutes instead of only forty seconds, several other children had to forfeit their time for that hour.

The result was a shift away from an interdependent, interactive classroom to a teacher-dependent model. In one-room schools, the teacher had given students assignments *at their own levels* and later checked out their mastery. In that class there were students of different chronological and developmental levels who received the work they were ready for rather than the work the teacher was ready to present. Now, however, the teacher prepares and presents the lessons, often lecturing, instructing, explaining, and moralizing. Children are frequently taught through rote and recall to regurgitate what the teacher has given them—which is not what we call effective learning!

There is a possible antidote to the steady diminishment of dialogue and collaboration at school. That is the increase at home of those activities necessary to encourage growth and learning in young people. Unfortunately, widespread changes in lifestyle have almost eliminated these activities in the majority of families, resulting in a society-wide drought in the critical ingredients of dialogue and collaboration.

Research is now confirming that dialogue and collaboration form the foundations of moral and ethical development, critical thinking, judgmental maturity, and teaching effectiveness. Conversely, lack of dialogue and collaboration between the more mature and less mature threatens the bonds of closeness, trust, dignity, and respect that hold society together.

As a result of the scarcity of dialogue and collaboration in homes and schools, a serious crisis has arisen in American culture. When adults lecture, instruct, explain, or moralize as their primary teaching methods, young people turn away, running instead to their peer groups as their primary source in their learning and identity-forming activities.

When peers dialogue with peers, all they achieve is naive clarity. *Peers* are "those at the same level of insight, awareness, and maturity." By definition, young people are incapable of informing themselves of all they need to know to become mature adults. How could they possibly alert themselves to the need for learning that of which they are completely unaware? It is only when more mature people—siblings, parents, relatives, teachers, neighbors, and other community members—collaborate with young people in learning situations, and then through dialogue encourage them to develop and clarify their thinking, that young people mature and gain a sense of discernment and judgment. (Later we will talk about how family meetings and class meetings provide children with opportunities for dialogue and collaboration through communication and problem-solving skills.) By the early 1960s, our young people were observably less mature and more vulnerable in the areas of moral and ethical development, critical thinking, and judgmental maturity than their counterparts in earlier decades. The closeness and trust in their relationships with parents and teachers were notably weaker, and they were far more tightly bonded to their peer groups than were children of previous generations.

THE OVERALL IMPACT

TABLE 1.1 SUMMARIZES THE CHANGES that have significantly affected the family and the development of young people. These changes have been so dramatic and so rapid that typical family patterns have been unable to accommodate them; hence, traditional child-rearing practices no longer adequately meet the needs of a majority of young people. However, adults who understand the significance of these losses are in a position to plan activities that will help children become successful people. They can do this not by going back to the old ways but by finding new ways to apply the principles by which human beings become capable. Such activities are offered in detail in the following chapters.

Table 1.1 Major Transitions in Lifestyle

Characteristics	Norm 1930	Norm 1980
Family interaction	High	Low
Value system	Homogeneous	Heterogeneous
Role models	Consonant	Dissonant
Results and consequences	Experienced	Avoided
Intergenerational associations	Many	Few
Education	Less	More
Level of information	Low	High
Technology	Low	High
Nonnegotiable tasks	Many	Few
Family work	Much	Little
Family size	Large	Small
Family dominant	Extended	Nuclear
Step-/blended/single-parent families	Few (10–15%)	Many (35–42%)
Class size (K–12)	18–22	28–35 students
Neighborhood schools	Dominant	Rare

2

Lost in the Shuffle

I T I S E A S Y for us as a society to look with nostalgia to the past, calling it the "good old days." Certainly, there is much to be learned from the past, as we ascertained in the preceding chapter. Nevertheless, objectively speaking, the good old days had negative as well as positive attributes, and it pays to assess the past critically to learn from it. Rather than looking back with dreamy nostalgia, we need to ask specific questions to determine what factors in the past facilitated the development of capabilities in children. Then, we need to find contemporary methods to implement these factors today.

In the preceding chapter, we identified the opportunities for developing capabilities that were lost to young people. Each such lost opportunity was like a grain of sand shifting from the positive to the negative side of a scale. With the decrease of weight on the positive side and the increase on the negative, the culture began to shift from one that gave nourishment and support toward a less stable, high-risk environment.

Still, we should not despair of the present situation. Only a relatively small number of compensations are required to restore the balance and create a healthy environment. In this chapter, we will pinpoint the four essential elements of culture that were compromised cumulatively and collectively in the previously described great urban shift. Also, we outline some of the responses that are already being made to restore the balance.

CRITICAL FACTORS

FOUR MAJOR FACTORS DEMAND OUR attention if we are to restore the dialogue, collaboration, and basic training in capabilities for young people. These factors, now missing to a significant degree in our culture, are:

1. networks
2. meaningful roles
3. on-the-job training for life
4. parenting resources

Networks

As a nation, we began our journey as hardy, self-reliant rural people who believed that discussing family and personal matters with strangers was unacceptable. However, in the world of the past, one had to go a long way to find a stranger. Nearly everyone within one's immediate frame of reference was at least an in-law. Conversely, today we must go a long way to find a relative, and in the new, urbanized interactive style even next-door neighbors are often considered strangers. How many of you know your neighbors, and how well? Do you know their names? Do you know what is going on in their lives? Or, do you simply smile and wave as you pass each other coming and going in and out of your remote-control garage doors?

In all of history, we are the first parents to raise and educate an entire generation of young people without the active involvement of networks of grandparents, aunts, uncles, cousins, nephews, neighbors, in-laws, and friends.

Another way of describing this situation is to say that we have lost our social networks. As a result, our children, bereft of a multiplicity of adult role models, have turned to peers for behavioral points of reference. This has created a distortion in values and an impediment to the process of maturity and responsibility that leads to well-functioning adulthood. Fortunately, we can learn to change this situation by making friends with our neighbors and creating the kind of social environment that once arose spontaneously within the extended family. It is likely that the greatest impediment to network building is the common belief that support groups are for people with problems. In fact, the opposite is true: Serious problems today are most likely to arise among people with no access to support groups.

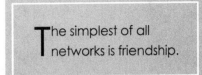
The simplest of all networks is friendship.

We need to transcend the kind of thinking that deems support groups only for the "needy" and become the kind of people who, as a matter of course, discuss and explore issues with those we work with, see at the market, and live around. Merely by talking openly, we will develop a large network of resources in a very short time.

Why is such support necessary to child rearing? Both young people's involvement with gangs and the incredible power of the peer group as we know it today tends to stem from the fact that peer groups (or peer-group surrogates in the form of rock groups) are now the validators and support systems of many of our young people. In these groups, young people feel listened to, taken seriously, and significant. Outside these groups, young people often feel lonely, discounted, and inadequate. Their families and teachers have been unable, in the new urban culture, to meet their basic needs.

In the past, if young people felt misunderstood or otherwise alienated from their parents or teachers, they could turn to their cousins, aunts, uncles, and grandparents for guidance. Because these family members shared the same family values and the same belief systems as the parents, they acted as a support network that reinforced the family's basic values. Thus, young adults had an outlet to vent their frustrations without going offtrack. Today, we need to re-create the same support system by creating supporting networks.

We can define a network in the simplest sense as two or more individuals who engage in dialogue about the world and the life they are living and who occasionally collaborate to achieve some mutually desirable end. Given this definition, the simplest of all networks is friendship. Networks can increase in complexity to comprise, at the most highly complicated end of the spectrum, elaborate civil defense and military systems in which people share information and data and work together to achieve some outcome. But for young people, the fundamental network was the extended family. This support was necessary for the stable development of young people.

Networks are essential to human social functioning. In the absence of a network culture, it is essential to actively learn to create substitutes for those that originally occurred spontaneously.

People are basically tribal creatures. Human beings have never done well in isolation, but they excel when they collaborate, teach, affirm, and encourage each other. Historically, networks—starting with the family and succeeding upward in complexity to vastly complicated organizations and institutions—have provided the forums in which we test and validate our roles and our assumptions and share our collective wisdom. In that way, we learn from the experiences of others. But as traditional networks disappeared in the rural/urban transition, people became more isolated. We were forced to rely on our own limited base of experience. This made it much harder to have any real sense of perspective or confidence about how to function as parents and family members.

Frequently, couples feel isolated and vulnerable. Many find that they turn inward on each other, hoping their partners will offset their insecurity. This overreliance between spouses often erodes the marriage relationship. Moreover, children frequently become objects of frustration and challenge to parents who do not have the resources to cope with them. In short, the growing lack of social support puts increasing stress on families.

Networks are essential to human social functioning. In the absence of a network culture, it is essential to actively learn to create substitutes for those that originally occurred spontaneously. Networks with relevance for our time are many. They include neighborhood crime watches, parent support groups, systems that enable parents to check with other parents, and personal growth groups.

Neighborhood crime watches consist of people who have declared themselves involved in their neighborhoods and are willing to talk to people about their concerns. By means of such networks, we have already done more in five or six years to curtail urban crime than we did by spending billions of dollars of federal and state money. Government efforts at controlling local crime could not succeed until people began to say, "Since I live here, I need to be involved. I am willing to talk with people at the supermarket. I will take the time to call the parents of my children's friends and check things out. If I see something happening at a neighbor's home, I won't just let it go. I am willing to speak out about it." This kind of concern and cooperation has had a great effect in improving the safety and stability of our neighborhoods.

Other effective grassroots networks have helped young people stay drug free. The National Federation of Parents for Drug Free Youth, formed in 1979, encouraged locally initiated awareness and networking programs. The White House highlighted and promoted the federation's work, and as a result, more than ten thousand local groups now actively talk, share awareness, encourage, and present programs to help and support young people.

Networks formed out of concern for teenage drinking have made a significant impact on a deadly problem. Over the Christmas holidays of 1984 and 1985, fewer young Americans died because of drinking than in any year since 1949. Examples of such programs are Safe Homes, Safe Rides; Chemical People groups; Families in Action; Parents Who Care; and Young People for Drug-Free Lives. Such networks composed of people collaborating and engaging in dialogue about issues in their environment are generally credited with turning the teen-drinking trend around.

Networks begin on a simple level close to home. For example, we can learn to call our neighbors and let them know when we are going to be away for a few days so they can keep an eye on our homes. We can encourage neighbors to watch out for our children and let us know whether they are getting into trouble—while we promise to do the same for them. And we can learn to see these reports not as criticism but as support.

Steve's family recently had an experience that forcefully brought home the importance of establishing an identity among people in the neighborhood. His daughter, Keri, left home in the family car to run some errands. She was traveling at highway speed down a narrow road when the right front tire of the car blew out and hurled the car into a narrow bridge. The car was completely demolished. Keri was pinned in the wreckage and had sustained sufficient damage to her face and body that she was in danger of suffocating.

The first person on the scene recognized the car and knew who owned it, since the family had made a point of visiting all the neighbors on the road upon first moving to the area. This person sent out a call for Keri's mother, who arrived immediately. She peered into the wreckage and saw that her daughter was suffocating. She realized that she was the only person there who was small enough to crawl into the wreckage to clear out Keri's air passages and keep her breathing, and she did so while others carefully began to cut the girl out of the demolished car. At the hospital, Keri's mother was told that even a few more moments without oxygen would have resulted in permanent brain damage or death for Keri.

It was simple networking that enabled Keri's mother to arrive in the nick of time. Only a few minutes determined life or death for Keri, and without the neighborhood network that was in place, those few minutes might have been used up in the efforts of strangers to find out who Keri was.

This experience reinforced our belief that when children associate with other children, it is important for the parents to become acquainted, develop an identity, and exchange phone numbers and addresses. It's simple to stop in at someone's home and say, "I see you are new in the neighborhood. I want to introduce myself and my children to you and meet your children." It is the beginning of an insurance policy against the kind of isolation that can have disastrous effects.

An understanding of the need for networks is now becoming apparent in many areas of our society. Religious institutions, which once provided pastoral counseling on an individual basis as their primary family service, are today open most nights of the week as community centers. Today, it's not uncommon for them to host such networks as Big Brothers and Big Sisters, Alcoholics Anonymous and Al-anon meetings, community forums, parenting classes, and singles groups. These churches have become centers for the extended family.

The business world has long recognized the importance of networking. Professional associations, conferences, and meetings with consultants are all designed to share new insights and information. When it comes to our families and children—which is our business as parents—it makes sense also to apply networking.

The parental equivalent of a business organization may be a parent group that meets in a church, temple, or neighbor's home. Neighbors can start monthly neighborhood meetings or block parties where they make it a point to discuss child rearing and what it really means when their children say, "Every one else gets to do it." Single parents can start support groups to share encouragement and exchange child care weekends. Parents could invite teachers to dinner, and schools could sponsor spaghetti dinners at which neighbors can get to know each other and their children.

In addition, we can learn to use the telephone as a tool for networking. We should not hesitate in calling another parent to say, "Since our children are spending time together, I thought it might be productive for us to talk and share a few ideas. What have you heard about the event coming up this weekend?"

In the last few years, it has been thrilling for us to see schools and communities progress from isolation to active collaboration through community partnerships, support groups, and other initiatives. Whereas in earlier decades school and parental interaction was the exception, today we see large numbers of parents and community people attend and participate in school programs and schools actively involved in community networking. Wise people are collaborating, building networks, comparing notes, and sharing responsibilities. Recent experience demonstrates that this kind of cooperation substantially reduces the considerable risks of family isolation.

Meaningful Roles

We are the first modern society to attempt to raise and educate young people who, until they become adults, have no role to play in the well-being of the family and community. These young people, over four million of whom are born every year, arrive in a society that no longer offers the stability of rituals, traditions, rite-of-passage experiences, culture, and activities that validate and reinforce their roles as contributing citizens.

From the cradle to the twentieth year of life, most children in America are on hold, receiving messages such as "Keep your mouth shut," "Stay out of trouble," "Get good grades," "Do what we tell you," and "Appreciate what we do for you." They seldom have experiences or hear messages that convey "You are absolutely critical to the survival of our family. We need you. We could not accomplish what we do without your participation." Is it any wonder, then, that many young people feel frustrated, resentful, and insignificant?

A primary reason for the decline in motivation, discipline, and achievement in schools is a lack of focus, direction, and ownership among young people. Most students have the general perception that whether or not they show up, things still will go on without them. In other words, their contribution is irrelevant. They are not used as teacher's aides in one-room schoolhouses as their progenitors once were. Nor are they active collaborators with their teachers in forging their own education. Most of their work represents the passive fulfillment of someone else's plans or ideas. They feel that their significance lies only in acquiescing to the demands and wishes of others and that society has little need for their unique contributions.

> Today we need to deal with our young people actively in ways that cause them to believe they are significant contributors rather than just objects or passive recipients of our activities.

In some respects, they are right. Very often when young people become assertive, even exuberant, they are viewed as a threat. Research shows that teachers see verbally active, assertive, creative students as a liability in the classroom. It is far easier for them to face a group of passive, quiet, docile students. Being treated as a burden or as insignificant when one is active, creative, and enthusiastic is hardly an affirming experience.

One of our favorite cartoons depicts Lucy asking Linus whether he enjoyed school. Linus replies, "I didn't go. I mean, I opened the door and shouted, 'Does anyone in there need me?' No one answered so I went home." The cartoon is funny. The reality is not. Children need to feel needed.

The cost of our failure to affirm our children's value as individuals has been profound. In 1995, as in every year since 1963, the data show that adolescents who attempted suicide generally did so in a period of their life when they had intense doubts about their personal significance and worth in primary relationships. This is reflected in U.S. society in an unexpected way. In 1940, approximately 70 percent of all babies born out of wedlock to adolescents were offered up for adoption. In 1996, the vast majority of babies born to adolescents were kept by their mothers, even though over 20 percent were under sixteen years of age. The incentive to keep the babies often reflects in large part the belief that a baby would love them unconditionally, need them, give their lives focus, and make them feel needed and significant. This belief is reinforced by a curious quirk in society: As soon as an adolescent becomes a mother, she is more likely to be treated as a woman rather than as the child she still is. She is taken seriously and often gains financial resources of her own.

A significant aspect of adolescent sexuality is the fact that some young people will compulsively engage in sex with people they hardly know (and sometimes they don't even like the person or the sex very much). In such cases, sex has been shown to be a strategy these young people use to make themselves feel significant, at least temporarily, in the eyes of someone else. "It is better to be considered important for my body and my sexuality than to be insignificant altogether" is the rationale they might articulate.

Today we need to deal with young people actively in ways that cause them to believe they are significant contributors rather than just objects or passive recipients of our activities. To achieve this, we must find ways to reorganize school and family dynamics that allow our children to play important, contributing roles.

Many families are learning the importance of family meetings, rituals, and family service projects as strategies to meet this need. Teachers are finding that class meetings, service learning projects, student mentors, and so forth, dramatically change the school climate for the better. In addition, the 1990s saw a great increase in young people, including college students, seeking out opportunities for volunteerism.

These trends are healthy and exciting because as children find meaningful roles in society, they develop a sense of importance and personal significance. By listening to our children, taking them seriously, and treating them as significant, we can restore a base of dialogue and collaboration that links them, us as parents, their schools, and their communities into a whole, thus giving them the very clear message that they are an important part of the whole that we call society. In subsequent chapters we will offer detailed guidelines for meeting this need.

On-the-Job Training for Life

For the first time in history, a generation of young Americans is receiving its impressions about life more from the media rather than from hands-on involvement with relevant activities. Generally, this perception of "reality" is deficient in teaching the skills of patience, personal initiative, hard work, and deferred gratification. On the contrary, in the world of television, issues surface and find resolution and results are achieved instantly, often by "heroes" who are sometimes psychopathic rebels, who achieve their objectives by violent, antisocial means. On television, self-medication, drinking, casual sexuality, acts of violence, and miraculous solutions to problems are the most common strategies for dealing with life.

It is important to focus on the actual content of the shows children watch on television, sometimes for hours at a time. Essentially, five premises are portrayed over and over.

The first premise is that drinking or substance abuse is the primary activity in productive social relationships. *The Breakfast Club,* an immensely popular movie in the 1980s, gave the clear impression that even the most intelligent young people could not have a good time until someone brought out marijuana and alcohol.

The second theme is that self-medication is the primary means of eradicating pain, discomfort, and boredom.

The third premise is that casual sexuality is the accepted norm. Time and again, this premise is demonstrated in the ease with which people flow in and out of relationships and beds.

The fourth premise conveyed by television is that acts of violence and lawlessness are acceptable solutions to problems. Characters lash out or make grand gestures toward themselves or others to manipulate circumstances. For example, they make suicide threats to get attention from the family or simply take another's car when they are in a hurry. Many television "heroes" would think nothing of breaking, entering, and taking the property of someone else to achieve some goal of their own.

The fifth premise is acted out primarily in commercials. It says that patience, deferred gratification, personal initiative, and hard work are unacceptable activities to be avoided through drinking, self-medication, or the use of some product or service. For example, a commercial for a familiar coffee suggests that any stressful, real-life issue or situation, such as the lack of intimacy and warmth in a marriage, can be cured immediately by the coffee in question. The coffee, the commercial suggests, is grown in special mountains, and when brewed up and served, it makes people warm, affectionate, and accepting. Thus, intimacy, warmth, and acceptance are portrayed as accessible through a commercial product. With multiple exposures to such suggestions, young people often come to believe them.

These five premises have increasingly found their way into the view many young people have of society. Children expect their late adolescence and early adulthood lives to conform to what they see on television, and thus they grow up with distorted expectations. And when those expectations chafe against real life, too many young people are at a loss for what to do.

As parents, we often compound the problems created by television messages by our example. By giving in too easily, we teach that most desires for material possessions can be realized not through hard work but through badgering, manipulating, and just plain wishing.

Dr. Bob Dupont, former head of the National Institute on Drug Abuse (NIDA), speaking at a Parents Resources in Drug Education (PRIDE) conference in Atlanta, Georgia, asserted that by failing to introduce young people systematically to the ways in which they affect their environment and to the needs for patience, self-discipline, and hard work in accomplishing goals, we actually set them up for the appeal of drugs. Drugs, he pointed out, produce instant, miraculous results in much the same way that hassling, manipulating, and wishing do, when parents are permissive. In both cases, the results are short term, never offering lasting gratification. Nevertheless, young people become conditioned to seek the path of least resistance and quickest means of getting needs met instead of through more valid but difficult methods.

Fortunately, many parents are learning how to manage the influences of television effectively. They are also learning how to structure the environment and family process to encourage the development of essential life skills such as self-discipline, judgement, and personal responsibility. Many schools offer life skills as part of the educational program. When properly designed, these programs are making invaluable contributions to the healthy development of young people. Apprenticeship, job shadowing, and mentoring programs in the workplace are developing as wonderful opportunities for young people to gain on-the-job training for life. We will discuss aspects of these strategies in subsequent chapters.

The Price of Affluence   Perhaps you have never thought of yourself as an affluent parent and therefore consider the problem irrelevant to your situation. If you have any doubts about meeting the criteria for affluence, try answering the following questions:

1. Do you have several pairs of shoes?
2. Do you have several choices about what you will eat for each meal?

3. Do you have access to an automobile for your personal transportation?
4. Do you have several sets of undergarments?

If you answered yes to three or more of these questions, then by the overall standards of the world, you are affluent. The majority of all people on earth will not be able to answer yes to three or more of these questions at any one time in their lives.

We talk about which pair of shoes to wear when a third of the people of the world have never owned any shoes at all. We talk about what to eat today when a major cross section of the world population wonders whether it will eat more than once during the day and is grateful for the same food every single day. We talk about securing our own means of transportation, even buying cars for our children, when at least half of the people in the world walk everywhere and can only fantasize about having a vehicle at their disposal.

Because these advantages have come easily to us, we often have little respect or appreciation for them. Moreover, by providing so much for our children without teaching them the means of achieving these things and respect for those means, we might be literally threatening their chances to survive through adolescence. Young people are led to believe that shoes, food, and cars will come to them automatically and that hassling, manipulating, and wishing will guarantee that they will be able to "go first class." In 1995, this kind of thinking resulted in an adolescent death toll that was comparable to the number of U.S. soldiers killed during the entire Vietnam War.

> Overall, on-the-job training for life includes increasingly complex lessons in patience, self-discipline, deferred gratification, personal initiative, sacrifice, and hard work.

In the eight years of U.S. involvement in the Vietnam War, about 56,000 war deaths were reported. In 1995, in just one year, most of nearly 50,000 adolescent deaths in America could be attributed to the kind of deficient on-the-job training discussed earlier.

Approximately 20,000 of these deaths were accidental, and in close to 12,000 of them, drinking were a major factor. In the same year, nearly 7,000 adolescents committed suicide in the United States (this figure has been adjusted to account for underreporting, which is chronic in figures on suicide). About 6,000 were the victims of homicide—the highest rate of youth-initiated homicide in history. Research indicates that a significant factor in increased homicide is the impact of alcohol on immature systems in the brain. It impairs impulse control and feelings.

Approximately 3,000 of the adolescent dead that year were the victims of domestic violence. We believe that a large cross section of this violence resulted from a lack of the support systems, networks, and awareness that would have helped to alleviate family stress. Close to 3,000 of the 53,000 died from the complications of pregnancy, abortion, or related health problems in young bodies not yet ready to bear children, practice abstinence, or engage in safe, responsible sex. More than 840,000 adolescents were reported missing in 1995, and more than 300,000 of these were missing for an extended period. By the end of the year, about 125,000 were still missing, and it is estimated that in a normal year approximately 14,000 of those in this category, called the long-term missing, are actually dead.

Add up the figures for yourself: 20,000, 7,000, 6,000, 3,000, 3,000, 14,000. Approximately 53,000 young people died in 1995, in part owing to our preoccupation with materialism at the expense of relevant, validating practice in patience, self-discipline, delayed gratification, sacrifice, and hard work—the values that would prepare young people to understand the nature of the choices they make.

Effective parents do not use their means (large or small) to provide too much, too soon for their children. Nor do they stay up all night doing school projects for their children. The most effective parents are those who let their children "pay dues" of time, effort, and accountability on little things now, to avoid much larger costs of such lessons in the future. Such small charges might inconvenience or upset them but will not hurt them. Overall, on-the-job training for life includes increasingly complex lessons in patience, self-discipline, deferred gratification, personal initiative, sacrifice, and hard work.

Affluence is by no means a requirement for effective child rearing. In fact, affluence in the form of indulgence can be harmful. The best way to destroy self-esteem and a sense of worth in young people is to do too much for them. This robs them of a sense of personal capability. The greatest gift of all is to help them validate themselves as agents in their own lives. We can do this by making them active participants in creating their own well-being and the well-being of others. In so doing we help them not only meet their own needs but also contribute meaningfully in meeting the needs of others.

Parenting Resources

The form of parenting many are faced with today is also unique in history. For the majority of children, it is performed by one or two inexperienced biological relatives, who usually work full-time and parent part-time. No longer can we rely on the collective contribution of several people of different levels of maturity working together to provide support through the first eighteen years of a child's life. Nowadays, fewer people with fewer opportunities struggle to get this critical job done. Simultaneously, children and parents are faced with more challenges than ever before in the form of drugs, drinking, sex, and dangerous, or at least ambivalent, messages from the media.

THE SIGNIFICANT SEVEN

EVERY HUMAN BEING IS BORN with the potential to become the world's most capable creature, not with the capabilities themselves. Unlike the amoeba, which is capable of functioning at its full potential from creation, humans acquire their capabilities primarily through apprenticeship: young human beings learn from those who have preceded them. When this apprenticeship is adequate, their toolboxes for life, which were empty at birth, are filled with the essential tools for effective living.

In times of change, these tools, which we call life resources, are particularly critical. For convenience we usually refer to these assets as "the Significant Seven." Ironically, researchers initially identified them almost by their absence. Insight dawned slowly as we reviewed research on those young people most likely to become clients of the criminal justice system, human services system, and social welfare system and those who failed to realize potential in school. Many of these people, we discovered, were those most poorly developed in these seven areas. Conversely, people who are living effectively and who were outstanding in many walks of life were characterized by unusual strength and adequacy in the Significant Seven.

More recent studies have focused on the quality of resiliency as a predictor of health, well-being, and the ability to thrive in the face of challenges and adversity. Not surprisingly, exceptional strength in the Significant Seven have surfaced again as characteristics of highly resilient individuals.

THE SIGNIFICANT SEVEN

Following are what we have been calling the Significant Seven:

1. Perceptions of personal capabilities

2. Perceptions of personal significance

3. Perceptions of personal influence over life

4. Intrapersonal skills

5. Interpersonal skills

6. Systemic skills

7. Judgment skills

Children and adults who are most at risk in behavioral health areas such as drugs, early pregnancy, delinquency, gangs, chronic academic problems, and so forth, are characteristically weak and/or inadequate in several if not all the Significant Seven.

Interestingly, research shows that people who have been living effectively but who become chemically dependent for any period of time normally regress in most of these areas. Once they are detoxified, the recovery process seeks to strengthen and/or rebuild the Significant Seven to help them maintain their recovery and begin to grow again.

In fact, it might be said that all children are born at risk to problems of dependency. The perceptions and skills that are necessary for self-reliance and effective living require development and maintenance.

Now consider the characteristics of low-risk individuals—people unlikely to fall into the known problem areas and likely to prove themselves successful, productive, capable human beings. They have developed the following:

1. Strong perceptions of personal capabilities—capable of facing problems and learning through challenges and experiences

2. Strong perceptions of personal significance—capable of contributing in meaningful ways and believing that life has meaning and purpose

3. Strong perceptions of personal influence over life—capacity to understand that one's actions and choices influence one's life and hold one accountable

4. Strong intrapersonal skills—capacity to manage emotions through self-assessment, self-control and self-discipline

5. Strong interpersonal skills—capacities necessary to deal effectively with others through communication, cooperation, negotiation, sharing, empathizing, and listening

6. Strong systemic skills—capacity for responding to the limits, consequences, and interrelatedness of human and natural systems with responsibility, adaptability, flexibility, and integrity

7. Strong judgment skills—capacity for making decisions and choices that reflect moral and ethical principles, wisdom, and values

A primary goal of parenting and teaching processes is that of strengthening these areas so that our young people can take on life with an adequate base of these personal resources and assets.

To comprehend the critical importance of this task, understand that young people who believe they are incapable and insignificant and that whatever happens is beyond their control tend to live life by default and reaction. They are generally exceptionally vulnerable sexually, chemically, socially, legally, and/or academically.

However, young people who strongly believe that they are capable of initiating learning and change in their lives, that their lives have significance, and that no matter what circumstances they encounter they have the capacity within themselves to influence how they respond and live in the face of them usually live by intent and action and are therefore much less vulnerable.

It is possible to help people in the first category to progress to the second at any time in life, but the younger they are when they develop a strong base, the greater the lifelong benefits. In the following chapters, we will explore what amounts to a shopping list of specific strategies to develop and strengthen these life resources in young people today.

3

Working with Perception

As noted earlier, four of the Significant Seven are essential skills, and three are critical perceptions. In this context, we define *personal perceptions* as the conclusions we reach about ourselves and our lives as the result of thinking through the experiences we have. Children are always making decisions about themselves (whether they are good or bad, capable or incapable), and thus about what they think they need to do to survive (sometimes called misbehavior) or to thrive (developing the skills for success in life). A *skill* is a capacity we develop and or learn to do as a result of practice and experience. While perceptions result from the thought process alone, it takes practice to acquire a skill.

Even though perceptions seldom have anything to do with truth or falsity, they are very powerful. For example, all human beings have worth, but people who perceive themselves as having no worth feel and act as if they are worthless. Adults can make a conscious effort to provide experiences that increase the chances that children will develop the kind of perceptions and skills that will serve them well throughout their lives.

Because perception forms the basis for comprehending the unique world of each individual, we are devoting an entire chapter to it. To work with people effectively, it is necessary to understand at least five aspects of perception:

1. Perceptions are keys to attitudes, motivation, and behavior.

2. Perceptions are products of four elements: experience, identification, analysis, and generalization.

3. Perceptions are cumulative.

4. Perceptions are unique.

5. Perceptions need to be supported and challenged to change.

As we examine each of these aspects of perception, it will become evident why working with perception is such an essential key to empowering ourselves and others.

PERCEPTION AS RELATED TO ATTITUDES AND MOTIVATION

IF WE THINK WE CAN, we will. If we think we can't, we won't. All that stands between ourselves and our capabilities are our perceptions of who we are and what we can do. The New Testament tells us, "As people perceiveth themselves in their hearts, so are they."

We sometimes believe that what we see determines what we think, but the opposite is true. What we think determines what we see. Pioneering psychologist Alfred Adler said, "Ideas have absolutely no meaning except the meaning we give them." Dr. Wayne Dyer has written an excellent book called *You'll See It When You Believe It!* that illustrates the power of belief in shaping humans' perceptions of reality.

Perceptual psychology, a field of study in which the understanding of the human psyche is based on that of human perception, holds as its central tenet the belief that whenever we perceive that something is possible in our lives, we experience a rebirth. This point of view has not always been widely received, but research is increasingly bearing it out. Psychology has evolved over the decades from the determinism of Freud, to the behaviorism of Skinner, to perceptualism as endorsed by the majority of psychologists today.

This sequence in the development of our present understanding of psychology echoes the course of human development. We come into the world as creatures of instinct (determinism). We then develop conditioned responses that allow us to anticipate immediate cause and effect (behaviorism). And finally we mature into perceptual human beings (perceptualism, which acknowledges the transforming power of perceptions).

We believe that perceptual psychology is the most relevant perspective for parents, counselors and teachers, as well as the most dynamic and optimistic, of all the schools of psychology. We applaud the research and the data that support this view and have based this book on the principles of perceptual psychology. The methods we offer to help adults work effectively with young people are firmly rooted in these principles.

While small children usually react in literal and concrete ways, normally developing human beings increasingly become creatures of perception. From about six to eight years of age onward, perception becomes a dominant force in determining what they do and how they live. Children can revise their

> All human beings have basic needs for potency, a sense of control over their environment, external appreciation for their perceptions and feelings, and affirmation of their significance.

histories, change their present circumstances, and transcend their parents and teachers—all by changing their perceptions. Parents who try to change children's behavior without changing their perceptions only encourage the expression of new behavior reflecting the firmly entrenched perception. For example, a child may "misbehave" because she does not have the perception that she is significant. Punishment only increases this perception—and the misbehavior. On the other hand, spending some "special time" with the child may change her perception of her significance and diminish the misbehavior.

For a number of years, adults have tried to intervene in the problems of young people through skill development—for example, with respect to communications and problem solving. However, this approach proved ineffective, because the young people they worked with inevitably returned to environments in which adults continually reinforced their negative perceptions of themselves and their opportunities. These perceptions translated roughly as "Why try? They won't give me a chance anyway. There's nothing I can do. Everything is up to fate or luck." Without perceptual change, the young people lacked the motivation to use their new skills and thus failed to change in any fundamental way.

This experience taught a basic lesson: The first task of parents and educators is to be sure that the learning environment fosters children's perceptions of themselves as capable, effective human beings. Otherwise they will have minimal effect on children on the level at which learning takes place.

All human beings have basic needs for potency, a sense of control over their environment, external appreciation for their perceptions and feelings, and affirmation of their significance. When these basic needs are blocked, people experience frustration.

People exhibit a number of potential responses to frustration. Strong, confident people confront a frustrating situation and change it. Less confident people, with that option closed owing to perceptions of themselves as inadequate, have two choices: (1) to fight their frustration through rebellion and resistance or (2) to flee into depression, withdrawal, and passivity.

It is critical for us to remember that perception is the key to attitude, motivation, and behavior. In other words, we need to deal with the *belief behind the behavior*—not just the behavior. If we don't change young people's perceptions, we will effect only temporary changes. Whenever we see behaviors, attitudes, and motivations that concern us, we must spend time studying them to find out how individuals' basic needs are being frustrated. Then, if we cannot change the conditions, we must work to change the perceptions that people have about those conditions and about themselves as experiencers of those conditions.

PERCEPTION AS THE PRODUCT OF FOUR ELEMENTS

OUR LEARNING MUST PASS THROUGH the following four levels if it is to permanently change the way we see the world:

1. The experience itself, which can come in many forms
2. What we identify as significant in that experience
3. Our analysis, based on our reason, of why it is significant
4. Our generalization, which results from our unique perceptions of what future value the experience has for us

A shorthand way of writing this list is *EIAG* or, specifically:

1. Experience
2. Identification
3. Analysis
4. Generalization

Professional educators have developed the EIAG acronym to help them remember the learning hierarchy. Another way of remembering it is to call it the What? Why? How? process. This process greatly enhances dialogue and strengthens relationships between adults and children when conducted in a climate of genuine interest and support.

We cannot overemphasize the importance of conveying friendliness and unconditional acceptance where learning is the goal. The following steps form guidelines in doing so while applying the EIAG formula:

1. *Experience:* Become aware of experiences, both negative and positive, in the young person's life.
2. *Identify:* Help the child identify the significant elements or outcome of a particular event.

Applying the EIAG process—whether in the classroom, the home, in counseling, or in personal relationships—enables us to help young people personalize their life experiences and develop their perceptions.

"What happened? What did you see? What are you feeling? What was the most important thing?"

3. *Analyze:* Help the person analyze why aspects of the event were important. "Why was that significant to you? Why do you think it happened?" However, since children are used to having teachers and parents using the question "Why?" against them, in some cases it might be less threatening to say, "What made that seem important to you? What were you trying to do? What caused you to feel that way?"

4. *Generalize:* Help the person discern from the experience a single principle that can be used in similar situations. "How can you use this information in the future? How can you do it differently next time for different results? What do you need to repeat if you want to achieve similar results again?"

By approaching the four steps of the EIAG hierarchy in this way, we can affirm and validate the perceptions of the young person we are working with. One of the most common errors in working with young people is to assume that they understand and interpret what they experience as a mature person would.

Applying the EIAG process—whether in the classroom, the home, in counseling, or in personal relationships—enables us to help young people personalize their life experiences and develop their perceptions. It also gives us some insight into how they interpret different events, which in turn helps us avoid the barrier of assuming, discussed later.

Steve's Story

Steve likes to cite the following story about his son, then six years old, to exemplify the EIAG process.

Because Steve traveled a great deal, he went out of his way to find opportunities for his son, Michael, to do things with him when he was home. Steve's goal was to help Michael perceive himself as significant and as contributing meaningfully to what they did together. One of Steve's strategies was to ask for Michael's assistance in fixing a tractor. The tie rod had broken and required welding. Steve outfitted Michael with some leather gloves and a welding mask so he could hold the parts in alignment while Steve did the welding.

After Steve finished the welding and began to put the tools away, Michael said, "Thanks, Dad, for letting me help you fix the tractor."

Steve reflected on his statement. It was obvious that he had appreciated the opportunity, but a perceptive listener would have realized that Steve had not achieved his goal. Michael did not come to believe he had done something important for his dad; rather, he expressed his belief that his dad had done something important for him. To help him understand the importance of his role, Steve knew he needed to check out Michael's perception of the experience and then help him reevaluate.

Steve's first step was to reflect back what he had heard: "Michael, I appreciate your thanks for letting you help me fix the tractor, but what you said tells me you may not have understood that I couldn't have done it without you."

His immediate response was "Sure you could, Dad. You can do anything."

Steve had forgotten what it means to be six years old and to look at your father, who solves all the problems and fixes everything. From his point of view Steve was as potent as Superman. "Son," Steve said, "I appreciate your confidence in me, but there are some things that I just couldn't do without your help, and this was one of them."

He asked, "What do you mean, Dad?" Now he was more interested.

Steve reflected the question back: "Why do you believe I could have fixed the tractor without you?" Steve suspected the question was probably too advanced for him at age six, but how could he know what Michael was ready for if he didn't check periodically?

Steve's suspicions were correct. He had started a little high by asking Michael to analyze the situation and tell his dad what he thought. He was not defensive but expressed genuine confusion in his answer: "I don't know."

Steve followed with an easier, describe-type question.

Small children can often describe, but not interpret, and adults can then usually build an interpretation out of a description. So Steve's next question was "Well, what was it you had to do?"

He understood that question. "I had to hold the tie rod together."

Steve said, "And what was it I had to do?"

Michael said, "You had to do the welding."

Steve asked, "How many hands did it take to keep the tie rod lined up?"

He said, "Two."

"And how many hands did it take to do the welding?"

"Two."

"Well, if it takes two hands to hold the tie rod, and two hands to weld it, how many hands does it take to fix the tractor?"

Michael said, "Does math have something to do with this?"

Up until that moment, Michael believed that math was something grown-ups used for persecuting small children. But suddenly math had become exciting since it had something to do with fixing a tractor. Steve remained silent, waiting for him to use the perception.

Suddenly he said, "It takes four."

"Well, if it takes four hands to do the job, how many do you have?"

He said, "Two.

"How many do I have?"

"Two."

Steve said, "Could either of us have done this job alone?"

Michael said, "No way, Dad."

He was excited now and asked, "Why does the tractor keep breaking in the first place?"

Steve said, "Well, Son, when I'm out doing the bush hogging and I'm driving along watching where the bush hog is going, I don't always see stumps in the grass. When the tractor hits them, sometimes they break the tie rod."

He said, "Dad, you know how it takes four hands to fix the tractor? Doesn't it take four eyes to drive it, too?"

Steve was overwhelmed with his insight. He thought for a moment and then said, "You're right, Michael."

He went on. "Well, I bet I could help you keep from breaking it just like I helped you fix it. But not if I had to sit back where you sit. I wouldn't be able to see the stumps, either."

Steve asked, "What would we have to do so you could help me?"

He said, "We would have to build a seat and put it up here on the front so I could watch for the stumps."

So they built a seat, put a little seat belt on it, and fastened it to the front of the tractor. Then as they drove along, Michael would yell, "Stump!" and Steve would go around it. In two years they haven't broken the tractor once.

When people visited their ranch, Michael would tell them very quickly, "Dad used to break the tractor all the time until I took responsibility for the stumps."

After that, Steve seldom returned home without Michael handing him a list of things that need fixing on the ranch, tasks that take two people. What he learned from the tractor experience is that "When a job takes two, I am sometimes equal to my father, and that makes me very significant."

A few weeks after the tractor incident, Steve received a call from his teacher, who asked, "What have you been doing to Michael?"

Steve asked, "Why do you ask?"

She said, "Well, he used to just sit there, waiting for instructions. Now he's going around offering suggestions and helping people. Couldn't we go back to when he used to just sit there?"

Steve replied, "Well, look at it this way. It's easier to tame a fanatic than to put life into a corpse. Now that Michael believes he's important, he's looking around for opportunities to help. That's a whole lot better than having him sitting in the back, distracted and disinterested in what's going on. Why don't you see if you can develop a plan to utilize a six-year-old teachers' aide? You might, for example, tell him, 'Michael, I appreciate your help, but there are times when I need to do things with the class myself. At those times I'll say, "This is my time, Mike. If you want to help, listen thoughtfully and carefully. When I'm ready for you to help, I'll come over and test you out to see if you understand the lesson. If you have it, then you can go around and be helpful to others."'"

Michael became a little man who was motivated by the prospect of helping others. He would sit in the corner of the classroom, listening intently, and often ask, "Are you done yet? Check me out. I've got it."

If we analyze what happened, we find that the significant experience was being involved in fixing the tractor. Had Steve not discussed it, Michael would have perceived himself as no more significant afterward than he did before. But when Steve helped him explore what was significant in that experience as he understood it (identify), why it was a significant contribution (analyze), and how he could learn from that experience to affect other things in his life (generalize), his perception changed. And the new perception supported this conclusion, the product of pure learning: "When I can find some place where my efforts are needed and important, I am significant." The difference between fixing the tractor and Michael's perception of personal significance lay in the three steps his dad took beyond the experience.

EIAG: A NATURAL PROCESS

SOME PEOPLE FEEL INTIMIDATED BY the EIAG process, claiming that it feels unnatural to stop and ask the what, why, how questions in a climate of friendly support. However, all of us use this process every day without even thinking about it. Suppose you have been wanting a computer but have hesitated to buy one because you thought it was too expensive. Then you notice an ad in the newspaper saying computers are on sale. As you scan the ad, you determine what in the ad is important for you: the computer. You ask, Why is the ad important? Because you need a computer and the price is right. Immediately your mind searches for how you can respond, and you begin to develop a plan to get yourself to the store.

> It is a misuse of the EIAG process to manipulate people into disregarding their own perceptions and accepting ours as the correct way of seeing things.

Every significant instance of learning in our lives has occurred by way of this process. But because the process is subtle, like breathing, we are usually unaware of it.

You do not need to struggle with this process, but you do need to be aware of its importance for real learning. Even in the classroom, it is not important to insist on going through every step with respect to every experience. What is important is our awareness that the perceptions of others are different from our own, that they are the keys to learning, and that it is our job to help young people explore their own perceptions to come to an awareness of their capabilities.

MISUSING THE EIAG PROCESS

IT IS A MISUSE OF the EIAG process to manipulate people into disregarding their own perceptions and accepting yours as the correct way of seeing things. The process should be used only in a genuine attempt to explore the perceptions of others. When this is your goal, the process comes easily. The questions "What?" "Why?" "In what way?" and "How?" arise spontaneously when your interest in the unique world of others is genuine. The key is to understand the child's perceptions—not to get the child to adopt yours.

Still, problems with EIAG can arise. One workshop participant told us that whenever she used the what, why, and how questions, her child simply responded, "I don't know."

Jane was able to share what she had learned from a similar experience:

When I first attempted this process with my son, I realized I was losing the spirit or purpose of the process. Instead of exploring his perceptions, I was more interested in wanting him to have the "correct" perceptions. I was not truly getting into his world.

I took Steve's advice to stop trying anything until I had learned to be a closet listener. When I quit focusing on my perceptions (and what I thought he should be thinking and feeling) and became quiet enough to give him a chance to talk at his own pace, he started opening up and sharing things of interest to him. He even shared a few feelings before I asked him any questions but simply conveyed a quiet attitude of interest and patience.

A closet listener never tries to force the communication process but concentrates on paying attention to what is actually going on. People communicate a great deal with their silences, their attitudes, their choices of where to place themselves, and even their bodily postures. And children tend to clam up when they feel threatened into doing something they don't want to do.

One mother arrived home from a workshop with great enthusiasm. She went straight to her teenager's room and said, "Is there anything you need to communicate to me?" This frontal approach traumatized the whole system; the boy simply shrugged and turned his back.

Think back to when you were a teenager. What were the implications of a question like the one this mother asked? "Did she find my stash? Did she go through my wallet and find incriminating evidence? Did she see me someplace

I should not have been? Does she have a specific answer in mind?" Most young people believe that the safest response to questions from adults is "I don't know."

But when you pay attention to people without letting them know you are doing it, you take the threatening quality out of your interest. Sometimes it helps to forget about the what, why, and how questions and simply work on establishing an attitude of genuine interest. Eventually, the questions will flow naturally from the feeling generated by that attitude.

When you patiently explore the what, why, and how with people, not to manipulate them into coming up with preconceived answers but to share the process of discovery with them, you can help them take meaning from their experiences as they think things through. Remember that it is not the event but how the person perceives the event that determines how he or she interprets it.

The EIAG process takes time and collaboration, so it is rarely used in typical home and classroom settings. Yet this process is essential for the development of critical thinking, moral and ethical ways of behaving, comprehension, and wisdom. It is in just these areas that we are struggling in our culture. If, as parents and educators, we can learn to be patient and use this process to increase dialogue with our children at home, we will be able to prepare them to offset the lack of dialogue typical of our crowded classrooms.

CUMULATIVE PERCEPTION

THE THIRD IMPORTANT FACT ABOUT perception is that it is cumulative. Most of us have had the experience of first reading a book and then, when we reread it at a later time, having significant new insights into its meaning. In the same way, perceptions yield new meaning as we mature.

We tend to grow, as the Bible says, line upon line, and precept upon precept. People who feel threatened in a learning environment tend to remain stuck if not given room to grow in small, cumulative steps.

Consider some of the things parents frequently say to their children. "How many times do I have to tell you? Surely you realize! Why don't you think? You are old enough to understand!" These judgments do not acknowledge the fact that perception is cumulative and that people move from one level to the next only in an environment of encouragement. Often we expect our young people to act on knowledge they have not encountered or assimilated. Instead of confronting the young with their inadequacy, it is important that we help them accumulate more wisdom while respecting their personal level of understanding and rate of accumulating more.

There are probably few parents alive today, including the authors, who will not feel some guilt at reading the prior comments. Therefore, we stress here and throughout this book that we are urging you not to become "perfect" in your dealings with young people but rather to increase your awareness and take small steps toward improvement. Guilt is useless if it lasts longer than ten seconds. Within that brief span, we can take note of your feelings of remorse and realize that they indicate ineffective behavior.

Sometimes one simply needs to start over. Some of us have to start over many times—frequently after we have waited to calm down (a topic discussed in chapter 11). In this back-up/begin-again process, the quality we need most is patience. We can gain it by realizing a simple but little-discussed fact: the one thing we cannot transfer to our children, ever, is wisdom.

Children have to accumulate wisdom for themselves. We can only help them do so; we can never give them wisdom by demanding and threatening that they take it. Mark Twain understood this process when he said, "When I was fourteen, it seemed to me that my parents did not know anything. By the time I was twenty-one, I was impressed at how much they had learned."

We can reduce our frustration when our children fail to be impressed with our wisdom if we remember that it is normal for adolescents to go through a know-it-all stage. During this period, when children are exploring their own perceptions and values, it is important to focus on those same perceptions and values, and explore them in dialogue. Otherwise, our children will perceive their parents as continually demanding and expecting qualities of them that they simply do not have.

PERCEPTIONS ARE UNIQUE

CONSIDER THIS ANONYMOUS QUOTE: "I know you believe you understand what you think I said. But I am not sure you realize that what you heard is not what I meant."

The lie most frequently told is "I know just what you mean." Knowing precisely what another means is impossible, for people's perceptions are as unique as their fingerprints.

No two people have ever read the same book. Nor has anyone ever read the book that an author actually wrote. Teachers make a mistake when they ask, "What was the point that was most important to the author?" rather than "What was your perception of what was important in the book?"

> To achieve understanding, we need to consider words in context and do quite a bit of clarifying through dialogue. Only then can we understand another person's perception.

Steve is a large, bearded, and bald-headed man, and he has stated that "every book I ever read had a bearded, bald guy for a hero." Jane sees the situation differently. "I always think the hero looks like Robert Redford," she says. Steve finds that perception quite incredible. "I always picture Robert Redford as the villain. I guess that's why I feel cheated when I go to a movie and see my favorite books tampered with. They always put a bald guy in the role of the villain, and the hero always looks more like Robert Redford or Tom Selleck. And that's just not the way I imagine the stories as I read them."

The point is that in reading a book, each of us has a unique experience based on his or her unique perception. Our own unique fantasy comes into play, and we see what we are prepared to see.

When people write books, they are recording their perceptions. When readers read those books, they pass them through their perceptions and add different emphases and meaning. Understanding this principle leads us to the reality that the time we spend foisting our perceptions on others is wasted. Our time is better spent by exploring the perceptions of the young people we try to teach. The following story illustrates this point very well:

A mother and father had gone away for the weekend, leaving their two children with a baby-sitter. On the Friday before they left, they had been to a doctor and learned that their five-year-old son needed to have his tonsils removed. While they were gone, this boy decided to hasten the process along. He removed the spring from his little hobbyhorse and twisted it firmly into his throat in an attempt to remove his tonsils. The baby-sitter had to rush him to the emergency room at the hospital to have the spring removed from his throat.

The mother was very upset when she returned and learned about this incident. When she talked with the boy later, she pointed out, "Putting that spring down your throat was a very silly thing to do, wasn't it, honey? See all the pain it caused you?"

The little boy said, "No, Mom, it wasn't silly."

Mom said, "Honey, it really was. It was a very silly thing to do."

The little boy insisted, "No, it wasn't silly, Mom."

Finally, a little bell rang in the mother's head, and she realized she was assuming the child's perceptions were the same as her own. It occurred to her to ask, "Honey, what does 'silly' mean to you?"

He answered, "Something that you laugh at, and this was nothing to laugh at, Mom. It really hurt my throat."

The English language can be ambiguous; many words have multiple meanings. To achieve understanding, we need to consider words in context and do quite a bit of clarifying through dialogue. Only then can we understand another person's perception.

Contributing to the difficulty are the built-in differences among human beings. From the moment two identical twins are laid in their bassinets, they begin to record varied experiences. One may see shadows; one may see light. But even when people see precisely the same things, each brings his or her unique interpretation to the experience. It is only through dialogue that each can begin to perceive the other's interpretation of what occurred.

Young people in particular are frequently unsure about how to interpret their experiences until they explore them with more mature people in a climate of support. Whenever we try to rush this process, however, whenever we demand more experience than they have had a chance to gather, then we both intimidate our children and help reinforce in them perceptions of their own inadequacy.

THE CLIMATE OF SUPPORT AND CHALLENGE

SUPPORT MUST PRECEDE A CHALLENGE when we want to motivate others to change. When people are challenged in an environment in which

BARRIERS THAT MAKE
INTERACTIONS THREATENING

1. An unwillingness to consider the validity of another person's point of view
2. The discounting or judging of another person's point of view
3. Blaming of others for one's own personal feelings (e.g., "You make me angry")
4. A lack of genuineness indicated by a tone of voice that contradicts the spoken message

BUILDING BLOCKS FOR
CREATING A CLIMATE OF SUPPORT

1. An openness to exploring another person's point of view
2. Listening with the purpose of understanding another person's point of view
3. Empathy, which results only from careful listening
4. A genuineness conveyed through warmth and interest
5. The ownership of personal feelings
6. Respect for differing points of view

they feel no support, all their energy goes into defending themselves—energy that could go into learning and changing.

Consider this message: "This is ridiculous. You know I love you." The dismissing, ridiculing tone cancels out the message of love. When we are truly loving, we don't see the perceptions of others as ridiculous. We seek understanding with "Honey, let me understand what caused you to see things that way." The attitude thus expressed is supportive and can be followed with a loving challenge: "Now that I understand, I would like you to reconsider another possibility."

The difference is clear. One response is supportive and shows a genuine desire to explore perceptions. The other is discounting and nonsupportive; it judges and then dismisses the perception of a loved one, thus diminishing him or her.

The EIAG process helps us avoid the barriers listed earlier. It is a supportive process that guides us in accumulating the insight necessary for exploring another person's unique point of view. For this reason, and many others that will become apparent, we will emphasize the EIAG process throughout our explorations together. We turn now to a detailed examination of the barriers to and building blocks for creating in our children strong perceptions of themselves as capable people.

4

Developing Strong Perceptions of Personal Capabilities

A BELIEF IN ONE'S personal capabilities is an essential building block for successful adulthood. The first of the Significant Seven deals with this issue.

In the eyes and attitudes of the parents and teachers who raise and educate them, children find mirrors in which they discover themselves. This principle is central to helping children learn to see themselves as capable people. Simply put, it is easier for children to have positive experiences in self-discovery when they spend time with people who consider them and treat them as capable.

Because children are motivated to learn and perform from birth, they can come to view themselves as capable at a very young age. Scott, for example, at eighteen months would constantly pester his mother to let him help. "Me do it," he would declare enthusiastically as he followed her around the house. He wanted to push the vacuum, dust the furniture, crack the eggs, and help with all the cooking.

"No, honey," his mother would answer. "You are too little to help me. Go play with your toys or watch TV now."

In this way, Mom had started undermining Scott's sense of capability very early, and Scott learned his lessons well. When he was ten years old, Mom would say, "Come into the kitchen and set the table." Scott would either ignore her or reply, "I'm busy playing with my games, Mom." Mom didn't realize he was only doing what he had been trained to do.

> Children want to help and to feel needed, and they want to do important jobs.

Children want to help and to feel needed, and they want to do important jobs. True, small children cannot vacuum or scramble eggs as well as adults can, but with training and supervision they can do an adequate job. Besides, the outcome of the job is usually not as important as helping children develop a belief in their capabilities.

Some parents may object: "But my three-year-old might burn herself if I let her scramble the eggs." This is true, but the chances of the child burning a finger are minimized when a parent has taken time to teach the child how to scramble the eggs. That parent could put the EIAG process to work here to explore the child's understanding of what could happen if he or she touched the hot stove or pan, why it would happen, and how to make sure it does not happen. Still, children under the age of six need careful supervision (though not interference) while scrambling eggs. With these practical precautions in place, a small burn is not as harmful to a child as the damage done when feelings of capability are lost.

What we need to do as parents is to take time to coach and mentor children. Then we can let them scramble the eggs, dust the furniture, unload the dishwasher, help with the shopping, and contribute to the household in other meaningful ways. Whenever we appreciate their contributions, no matter how small, we are helping them see themselves as capable people.

THE BARRIERS AND BUILDERS

FIVE DISTINCT BEHAVIORS THAT UNDERMINE self-confidence, reduce closeness and trust, and convey disrespect for children's worth and capabilities frequently occur between adults and children. These are the barriers to developing capable children. In the preceding chapter we listed these barriers briefly; here we explain them in more detail. The same is true for the builders—five behaviors that consistently affirm and validate young people and our belief in their capabilities. We cover them alternately with the barriers.

Remember that each barrier behavior reduces the capacity of a relationship to support, affirm, and encourage the less mature party and diminishes his or her self-confidence. When we do nothing more than eliminate these barriers, we experience a substantial improvement in all our relationships with children. When each barrier is replaced by a builder, we enjoy a much greater improvement in our relationships with our children.

Barrier 1: Assuming in Ways That Limit

All human beings require assumptions to function. Healthy assumptions are those that keep all options open. For example, when we assume that everyone we are involved with is a constantly growing and changing individual who has potential that even they may not be aware of, we usually approach them with openness and optimism, and we learn and grow together. However, when we assume what people will think, how they will respond, what they can or can't do, and so forth, we often create barriers.

The barrier of assuming is generally borne out of expediency. It saves time to assume how those we love and live with will respond to specific experiences and then to act in accordance with our assumptions. Have you ever said to someone, "I didn't tell you because I knew you would get angry"? Were you surprised that the person got angry for being kept from trying not to get angry? In another example, whenever Steve goes home, his mother says to him, "Don't forget your coat." The last time he forgot his coat he was eight years old; his mother assumes that no growth has taken place in fifty-two years.

If Helen Keller had been raised by parents who assumed that because of her blindness and deafness they had to do everything for her, she would have lived a very limited life, for her family had already assumed how little people with her impairments could do. It wasn't until Anne Sullivan came along and challenged these assumptions that Helen was given a chance to develop.

When we act on limiting assumptions, we ignore the most beautiful characteristic of human beings, which is the ability to learn and change from day to day. By assuming, we say, "What you were yesterday is all I will allow you to be today."

B. F. Skinner, the famous psychologist, showed that creatures such as rats repeatedly respond to the same stimulus the same way out of habit or instinct but that human beings respond to stimuli out of their beliefs. When a stimulus comes to the attention of a human brain, it passes through a belief system that produces a menu of possible responses. The brain then looks over the menu and, in accordance with the person's beliefs, selects or creates a behavior. However, as people proceed with the behaviors they learn from each experience, they may change their beliefs. Therefore, the same stimulus may produce a different response at a different time. For example, a spark pops out of the fireplace, and a person rushes over and steps on it with bare feet. Next time he will probably try other means.

If we want children to believe that they can grow and change, it's essential for us to reflect this belief in how we deal with them and what we model in our interaction with them. Perhaps a good question to ask before we assume is "What will happen if I don't act on this assumption now?" The answer is usually "I might discover new possibilities!" Whenever possible, it is better to assume nothing and discover than to limit through assumptions and discourage growth.

Think of how you feel when someone says "I didn't tell you about _____ because you always get upset!" You usually get "upset" about being discounted for your history! How often do we see couples and parents "beating hope to death with history"? "You always think _____!" or "What good would it do to try and talk to you about it!" or "Why can't you ever_____?" This could be called the language of the lost, and it is very reflective of how negative assumptions undercut encouragement and optimism about relationships, learning, growth, and change.

Steve has a fantasy of his mother deciding to be silent when she sees him walk toward the door, instead of assuming that he will still forget his coat like he did when he was eight years old. But he thinks he might give in to the temptation to say, "Aren't you going to remind me of my coat?" "No, dear," she would say, "I'm sure if it is important to you, you'll get it." Then Steve could say, "Well, I'd better get it, because it could get cold out there." And his mother would conclude with satisfaction that after half a lifetime he had finally learned how to look after his coat.

Builder 1: Checking

As an alternative to negative or limiting assumptions, try checking as a way to learn how much understanding people have and how capable they are. In addition, active checking aids us in helping them develop their perceptions and discover their capabilities.

To return to Steve's example, his mother could have said, whenever the question of his coat arose for her, "Honey, what kinds of things will you need to have with you on this trip?" and then if he doesn't think of his coat and it is important to her, she could say, "What kind of weather are they expecting in _____?"

When we take the time to check, we are saying that we respect the fact that the person is capable to make decisions and that we are trying to make room for his or her growth. Checking is the logical alternative to assuming, and it works to advantage in all relationships, not merely those involving parents and children. When we assume we know how our spouse or children will respond ("I didn't tell you because I knew you would get annoyed"), that assumption is disrespectful and always leads to anger and frustration. A more supportive alternative would be "Honey, I need to check something out with you" or "How would you like to handle ____?" That approach at least gives the spouse and/or child a chance to express his or her growth, capabilities, and understanding.

The rule of thumb is wherever possible to substitute dialogue and patience for assuming. Coach yourself by saying, "How can I use this situation to check out what this person knows, sees, is ready to learn, and can do?"

> Checking is the logical alternative to assuming, and it works to advantage in all relationships, not merely those involving parents and children.

Barrier 2: Rescuing or Explaining

Too often as parents and teachers, we step in prematurely to take care of something for children that they haven't yet learned to deal with for themselves instead of allowing them to learn through experience. Or we step in and provide explanations for them instead of helping them discover the meaning of an event for themselves.

There is a prevailing belief that good parents and teachers explain things to children. However, truly effective parents and teachers work with children to help them develop useful explanations for themselves. Explanations offered from the outside can be confusing. For example, have people ever started explaining something to you that they were quite familiar with but that you had never thought through before? Chances are, the longer they went on with their explanations, the more confused and frustrated you became.

Children feel intimidated whenever adults are too quick to step in and take care of or explain something for them. Our "brilliance" baffles them and leaves them feeling very vulnerable. What would happen, they might start to wonder, if we were not there?

People who step in too quickly to take care of things for others are called *rescuers* and *enablers*. They rescue people from their inadequacy and then enable them to remain vulnerable and easily manipulated. We hear them all the time: "This is what happened." "This is why it happened." "This is what you had better do to fix it." These statements imply "Shut up, dummy. If you would let others do things for you, you wouldn't have gotten into such a mess in the first place." Such statements do not encourage children to know that they are capable and significant.

We have talked with many newly married couples who have acknowledged their fear and uncertainty at suddenly being expected to begin budgeting, shopping, arranging health care, providing themselves shelter, and doing all the many things that had always been done for them at home. By consistently playing the rescuer role, their parents sent them out into the world unequipped with the tools necessary for adult life.

By stepping in too quickly to take care of something for others, we prevent our young people from having necessary experiences. And by stepping in too quickly to explain, instead of patiently inviting the children to think an occurrence through without a put-down, we prevent growth even when they had the actual experience. In either case, doing nothing, patiently, is far better and far more helpful than doing something prematurely.

Builder 2: Exploring

When we encourage or allow people to work on things and/or try to deal with them, we need to then follow up by asking questions such as "What is your understanding of what was happening?" "What might have caused that to happen?" "Having had that experience, how will knowing this effect the way you deal with this in the future?" We con-

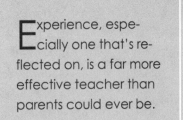

Experience, especially one that's reflected on, is a far more effective teacher than parents could ever be.

vey a belief in their ability to gain resourcefulness by trying new things and gain wisdom through problem solving for themselves.

Our patience in exploring experiences with young people conveys this message: "I see within you the capabilities to master situations and gain understanding. And rather than preempt you with my impatience, I will take the time to allow you to discover." Consider the following example, which Jane experienced with her daughter, Mary:

Mary forgot her lunch. The school secretary allowed her to use the phone so she could ask her mother to bring it to school. When Mary's mother refused to bring her lunch to school, the school staff concluded that she was very cruel and irresponsible.

But Mary's mother was not interested in demonstrating her sense of responsibility. She was interested in helping Mary learn responsibility from her experiences, so she gave the school permission to let Mary walk home to get her lunch.

Mary was angry with her mother for making her walk home. Her mother put her lunch next to the front door and got into the shower. When Mary marched into the bathroom, ready to express her anger and try manipulating her mother into driving her back to school, her mother said, "Honey, I'm busy now. You'll need to hurry back to school. We can talk about it later."

After school, when Mom knew Mary had had time to cool off somewhat, she listened as Mary told her how embarrassed she had been because her mother would not bring her lunch to school. Then she asked Mary, "Do you know I really love you?"

Mary admitted that she did. Her mother asked, "Do you know I really want what is best for you?"

Mary said, "When you won't bring my lunch to school for me when I forget it, it seems as if you don't care."

Mom said, "Honey, let's take a look at that. What happened to cause you to forget your lunch?"

Mary said, "I was in such a rush to catch the bus that I just forgot it."

"How did you feel about not having your lunch?"

Mary admitted, "I just wanted to have it. I was hungry."

Mom asked, "What do you think you could learn from that?"

Mary said, "Well, one thing I learned is that you won't bring it for me because you want me to be more responsible. What a drag! I suppose I could leave my lunch by the front door every day so I can grab it when I'm in a rush."

"Can you think of anything else?"

Mary thought a minute and then said, "Well, I could also get up as soon as my alarm rings so I won't be so rushed."

Mom joked, "Did you think I would deprive you of all that learning by bringing your lunch to school for you?"

Experience, especially one that's reflected on, is sometimes a far more effective teacher than having parents do it for you or explain their experience for you. When healthy children go out to play on a relatively mild day and if they forget their jackets, they will merely become uncomfortable. A rescuing parent would say, "Be sure to put on your jacket, dear. It is very cold out there." If the child went out without the jacket and came in cold, the explaining parent would probably say, "Now, you know you shouldn't be out there when it is cold. That was a silly thing to do." But a wise parent would let the child learn from the experience. When the child came in cold, encouraging parents would say, "Yesterday you were out playing and you weren't cold. What was different?"

"Yesterday I had on a jacket, and a hat, and gloves. Today I ran out in my T-shirt."

"If you want to keep playing out there without being cold, what things could you do?"

"Well, I guess I could get my jacket."

"OK. It is up to you, honey, if you want to be warm."

One mother told us she had never had much luck convincing her child to save her allowance for things she might want at the end of the week. She would try explaining to Lisa that she would be sorry later if she spent all her money on the first day, but Lisa would still spend it all early. Then her mother would say, "I told you so. Why don't you ever listen?" Every week the same thing would happen.

This mother was surprised at how little it took to get different results. On the next allowance day, when Lisa wanted to spend her money on a snow cone, Mom asked, in keeping with our suggestion, "How do you think you will feel tomorrow when your money is gone? Can you think of anything else you might want to have money for during the rest of the week?"

Lisa simply said, "I guess I don't really want the snow cone. I'm sure I will want something more during the week."

Said Mom to us, "I felt awkward asking these questions, and I wasn't even patient enough to wait for a response to my first question. But at least I started the process, and it encouraged Lisa to think for herself instead of asserting her independence by rebelling against my attempts to explain and rescue her from making mistakes."

The following story provides another example of effective exploring:

Mr. Hanson asked his child what he needed to have ready for his field trip on the weekend. When the boy answered, he noted some holes in the plan but none that could hurt his child seriously.

When he got back from the field trip, Mr. Hanson asked the boy how it went. "Not so great," said his son. "I was hungry and cold."

"Why?" asked Dad.

The child said, "I didn't have enough food, and I didn't take my jacket."

Mr. Hanson asked, "What would you do differently next time, now that you have had this experience?"

"Well, I think I would check the weather, and bring enough food for three meals."

Mr. Hanson's first step was to encourage his son by asking what he needed to be ready for the field trip. Then, after the experience, he used the builder of exploring rather than the barrier of explaining to confirm the value of the experience in the boy's mind—that is, to create a fruitful climate for learning. One step led naturally to the other.

Steve has a foster son who had a similar experience. After the boy returned home from a trip, Steve asked, "What was the most important thing you learned during the trip?" (expecting some great revelation).

He replied, "I was reminded about how much I hate bologna."

Steve asked, "What do you mean?"

He said, "That was all people were willing to loan me."

Steve said, "Well, given that, what do you plan to do on your next trip?"

He said, "I'm going to take a bucket of chicken for me and some bologna for the suckers who forget."

Using this builder helps children develop confidence in their ability to learn and engage in problem solving. These are foundations of decision making and mature judgment. By rescuing/explaining, we often undercut the development of our children's judgment skills as well as their sense of being capable.

Barrier 3: Directing

Directing is another of the behaviors born of expediency. It is much easier to step in and tell children to do things our way than to invite their participation and contributions and accept that they might do things differently. Human beings are basically very independent creatures who demand a certain level of respect for

their uniqueness. When we are overly or unnecessarily directive, we usually encourage hostility, aggression, resistance, and/or passive-aggressive behavior.

Think for a moment about how you feel when
supervisors or bosses insist on telling you how to
perform every detail of a task you are supposed to
have mastered. If they do this long enough, you
might start looking for another job; at any rate,
your motivation and willingness to cooperate will
drop off sharply. But when your bosses invite your
contributions with respect, you doubtless believe
that they feel you have something valuable to offer.

> Directing makes
> children feel impo-
> tent and frustrated. The
> more directive a parent
> or teacher is, the more
> rebellious and resistant
> children become.

Most of us, when we think about it, can see the
problems caused by being overly directive and con-
trolling, but we might still say to a child, "Pick that up. Put that away. It is
time for your shower. Be sure to drink your milk before the bus comes."
Children get even by making us feel frustrated and impotent, by resisting or
refusing to follow our directions. In fact, they will often go out of their way to
alter the task ever so slightly, just to assert their independence.

Directing can have a significant negative effect on family life and is probably one of the most widespread of all the barriers. It is always "easier to do it
myself" than to invite another to contribute and cooperate. On the other
hand, if we can find the patience to invite and encourage our children's participation and say, "Listen, I have some friends coming, and the family room is a
mess. If you could get it straightened up for me, it would really help me out a
lot," the results will be instantaneous. Shoes and socks will disappear from the
floor like magic and the room will be relatively orderly in no time.

Directing can make children feel impotent and frustrated. The more directive a parent or teacher is, the more rebellious and resistant children become.
One workshop participant brought a good example to one of our three-day
training sessions:

> *I always leave these lists of instructions for my husband and children
> and come home and find the family resentful and the instructions only fol-
> lowed halfway. I never understood why they're so hostile about it or why
> they are so resistant and uncooperative. Until I learned the effects of being
> overly directive.*

The first night of the training, I had an assignment for the next day and was asked to spend a couple of hours on it. But, I don't work that way! I have to always make sure that everything is exactly right and under my control! So I stayed up all night preparing for the next day. In the morning I was rechecking and lost track of time. All of a sudden I realized I was going to be late to the session. As I ran out the door, I said to my husband, "I have been so caught up in this training I haven't had a chance to orga- nize anything, and we have company coming tonight. If you get home be- fore I do, I'd appreciate anything you could do to help me out."

When I came home, food was cooking on the stove, the washing ma- chine was going downstairs, and my husband was vacuuming the family room.

"What's happened?" I asked, astonished.

He said, "I knew you were under pressure because you didn't have time to leave one of those darn lists I hate so much. As I've been vacuuming, I've been thinking, and it occurred to me that I lived successfully for thirty years before we married. I paid my bills, took care of the things I needed to do, entertained my friends, and organized my life, and I haven't received much credit for that since we married. In fact, I realized that I've been starting to feel toward you the way I felt toward my mother when she did this to me. And I finally left her for another woman!"

This story makes the important point that adults as well as children resist directing. In fact, all the barriers and builders have relevance to relationships of all kinds, not just parent-child bonds. As another example, we worked with a staff development coordinator for a major school district who was so limiting, controlling, and directing that she constantly reduced everyone in the system to the level of kindergartner. People's behavior toward her showed the resent- ment she inspired. At the end of the first day, she said, "I want each of you to pick up your cup and put it in this trash can before you go." One-third of the adult participants left their cups right where they were. These were school principals, superintendents, and other people used to having some authority, and they resisted her direction in the same way children would have done.

The next day we stepped in to model another kind of behavior. We said, "The school is going to have another meeting in here when this one is finished. They have asked us to be sure that things are in good shape when we leave. We would appreciate anything any of you who have an extra minute could do to help us get the room together."

The participants reorganized chairs, put on a fresh pot of coffee, cleaned the blackboard, and did everything that had to be done. By inviting their contribution and encouraging them to assist, we encouraged their extra effort. But by demanding and directing, the staff development coordinator had evoked only resistance and hostility, as she finally was able to see.

Whenever we are about to direct another human being, we can ask ourselves two questions:

1. "Will the world come to a screeching halt if I don't handle every detail of this transaction exactly my way—right now?" This is a slightly lighthearted way of asking whether any truly major, unacceptable consequences could arise if we allowed the other person the dignity of handling the transaction his or her way. If the answer is yes, then of course we should step in and handle it. If, however, the answer to this question is no (which it usually is), then we can ask the second question.

2. "Will this human being ever have to develop plans of his or her own in life?" If the answer is yes, then avoid needless directing and use the following builder. How do people learn to make plans of their own if they are never encouraged to plan something? How do they ever learn to confront flaws in their plans if they are never allowed to implement a plan with a flaw in it, or if they are made to feel so inadequate because of the flaw that they become fearful of trying again?

After all, our greatest successes in life frequently result from apparent failures that we embrace as learning experiences rather than taking them so seriously that we were afraid to try again. All this would suggest that directing should be our least desirable response to getting others to do things, chosen after careful consideration, not our first, knee-jerk reaction.

Builder 3: Encouraging/Inviting

In the previous examples, it is clear that whenever people are invited or encouraged to contribute, they are generally willing, cooperative, and responsive. Children feel encouraged when we see them as assets rather than objects, regard mistakes as opportunities to learn rather than as failures, and invite participation and contributions rather than directing and demanding compliance.

A teacher who says, "We are almost at the end of the class, so anything that you can do to help put the room in order for the next class will be greatly appreciated!" will get consistently more help from the students that one who says, "Do this . . . Move that . . . Don't forget to pick up _____!"

When you have a problem in how the family is handling things and you come home from work and say, "This is the problem, so here is what each of you needs to do in the future!" most members of the family will leave it up to you to make it work. A more successful approach would be for you to come home and say, "This is a problem that is facing us, so I would like everyone to give some thought to how we might deal with it and what each of you can do to help out. Then let's schedule a family meeting to work it out." Even though you may come up with the same solution, family members will generally take ownership for their part and make it work—because they were invited to contribute rather than directed to do what you told them to.

Steve's daughter Kristi teaches special needs children in kindergarten. Through the creative use of class meetings and her exceptional skills as a mentor and coach, she has a group of five-year-olds who have developed their own systems for getting the classroom straightened up; conducting class meetings; having a fun and orderly lunch period each day; helping each other with problems like coats, shoe laces, and itchy-scratchy things; and getting an exceptional amount of learning done each day.

While other teachers run around frantically trying to direct and supervise the children, Kristi serves as their consultant and guide as they get things done and learn to "supervise" themselves—because she invited their contributions and ideas and encouraged them to take initiative and find ways to get things done.

Barrier 4: Expecting (Too Much, Too Soon!)

"Shouldn't we have high expectations for our children?" you might ask. There is actually some debate on this question, because many parents are not certain about how to make expectations encouraging. Remember, as psychologist William Glasser has said, "People have a tremendous ability to live down to the lowest expectation in any environment. Define them as capable and treat them that way, and they will generally behave accordingly. Define them as inadequate or unacceptable and treat them accordingly, and they will justify your worst expectations."

High expectations in raising children are great as long as they are possibilities and opportunities viewed with anticipation, patience, and optimism. When they become standards by which we point out children's inadequacy or make them conditions for acceptance, we can create discouraging and destructive experiences. The barrier of expecting too much too soon is rooted in a lack of respect for the growth process and impatience with children's shortcomings.

To begin appreciating the potential harm in expecting too much too soon, consider the experience of many clergy who preach perfection as a standard and then in their sermons emphasize the members' failure to live up to it. They generally end up with a shrinking congregation of depressed masochists endlessly trying to bribe God (financially) into overlooking their lack of perfection. However, those clergy who preach becoming perfected as an eternal goal and then are quick to celebrate any apparent movement (however small) toward it by anyone and everyone in the congregation generally have an inspired, growing, excited congregation. Many of their members say, "I'm not where I'm going yet, but I'm not where I was! So every chance to grow and change is a blessing from God to be celebrated!"

Let's use an example of incremental learning. We expect our children to learn to make their beds, so we start out with something they can do. They have no problem straightening the covers. They can fluff up the pillows. Over time they will develop the full range of bed-making skills. So we celebrate their small achievements—"You got your cover and pillow straightened up today, and that's an important part of getting your bed made"—and encourage them to move on. That is the positive alternative to holding our expectations up to our children and demanding that they meet them.

We can and should have the highest possible expectations for those we love, but without engaging in expecting. Having high expectations means that we believe in the capabilities of our children, which we reinforce by helping them develop and realize through action.

Builder 4: Celebrating

Children are amazingly responsive to outside stimuli. When we are quick to celebrate any little movement in the right direction, we get more results. Celebrating is simply the act of recognizing progress: "Son, I appreciate the

When we are quick to celebrate any little movement in the right direction, we get more results.

fact that you straightened the cupboard and put the dishes in the sink." Notice that there are no buts to this remark; this is an unqualified recognition of achievement.

Many of us are fixated on buts. Whenever a compliment is given, we wait for the but: "Nice job on this and this, but. . . ." The qualifying statement destroys the value of the compliment and increases the receiver's sensitivity to criticism.

Too often, adults are preoccupied with what is not happening in a relationship and overlook what is. How many times have we seen a parent come home, ignore the fact that the cupboard was cleaned up and the dishes washed, and comment only on the fact that the trash wasn't taken out? When we focus on the negative and ignore the positive, we convey this message to our children: "It is better not to waste time and effort doing well, because my parents won't notice anyway. All they ever notice is what I don't do." Soon the child will say, "If I just ignore Mom altogether and do nothing, she will run around doing it herself while she is yelling at me. All I have to perfect is my ability to ignore the yelling, and I'm home free."

Remember, it is easier to tame a fanatic than to put life into a corpse. When we set high expectations and then point out people's deficiencies, we discourage them and create corpses that we have to pump up endlessly and carry along. But when we are quick to celebrate any little movement in the right direction, then we are affirming and validating the people with whom we are involved and often interest them deeply in doing more.

If we raise children to be independent, self-reliant people, they will be. Sometimes we put young people in a double bind by first steering them toward independence and then objecting to their way of doing things.

The author Garrison Keillor tells the following story:

> Our Sunday school class learned "Joy to the World" for the Christmas program. You asked me to sing it for the aunts and uncles when they came to dinner. I said, "No, please."
> You said, "Yes, please."
> I said, "No."
> You said, "Someday when I'm dead and in my coffin, maybe you'll look down and remember the times I asked you to do things and you wouldn't."

So I sang, terrified of them, and terrified about your death, and you stopped me halfway through; you said, "Now, come on, you can sing better than that."

A few years later when I sang the part of Curly in Oklahoma! *and everybody else said it was wonderful, you said, "I told him for years he could sing, and he wouldn't listen to me."*

But I did listen to you and that's most of my problem. Everything you said went in one ear and down my spine. Now you call me on the phone to ask, "Why don't you ever call us? Why do you shut us out of your life?"

So I start to tell you about my life. But you don't want to hear it. You want to know why I didn't call. I didn't call because I don't need to talk to you anymore. Your voice is in my head, talking constantly from morning until night. I keep my radio turned on, but I still hear you, and I will hear you all my life, until the day I die, when I will hear you say, "I told you."

Winston Churchill was raised with encouragement. He was not intimidated by errors. When he made one, he simply thought the problem through again. Someone asked him, "Sir Winston, what in your school experience best prepared you to lead Britain out of her darkest hour?"

Winston thought a minute and then said, "It was the two years I spent in the first form [seventh grade]!"

"Did you fail?"

"No," replied Winston, "I had two opportunities to learn to do it effectively. What Britain needed was not brilliance, but the will to persevere and the ability to improve on an initial effort that went poorly."

When we encourage children and invite them to explore possibilities, we help them develop positive attitudes toward learning from experience and even from seeming failures. Consider this example:

Steve's father experienced this double bind. When he was a child, his mother had told him, "You can't go swimming until you learn how to swim because you might drown." Throughout his childhood and adult life, this man tried and failed to gather the courage to learn to swim for fear he would drown. Not until he was a grandfather did he succeed in trusting himself in the water, after a group of his grandchildren contrived to wrap him in several water-ski belts and flotation jackets and let him hold a float while they pushed him into deep water. They filmed the whole event. It took fifty-three years and a group of innovative grandchildren ready to celebrate his success to overcome the binding negative expectations his mother had planted in him.

With celebration, timing is critical. The rule of thumb is to let the celebration of an improvement stand alone. At a later time we can say, "Honey, these dishes are getting in the way. I'd appreciate it if you would come in here and clear them now." Any improvements can be dealt with as a transaction separate from the celebration of improvement. When that is the case, children feel, "Boy, even if I don't get everything together, they notice and appreciate what I do, so it's really worth trying."

> We need to be encouraging to ourselves as well as our children, and celebrate our own incremental successes as we go through life.

The essence of the approach is to affirm anticipations (as distinct from expecting) and then to celebrate the fulfillment of the anticipations. Children can understand this message: "I expect you to become all you can, and I anticipate that you will meet my expectations in a series of small steps within your reach. Therefore, any time you take a small step, you have fulfilled my anticipations and have moved toward your potential. That is a reason for great joy."

A child who has never tried to wash clothes before and who one day takes the initiative and runs the washer with only a sweatshirt in it should not be criticized for wasting soap and water. The point is to celebrate what went right. Next time you can leave a few more clothes in a basket by the washer and suggest that the child include them. It's the increments that matter, not the overall performance.

Studies of successful, healthy people show that they are consistently good finders who see lemonade in lemons and glasses that are half full rather than half empty. Incidentally, such people, who are quick to celebrate any little movement in the right direction, have very few problems with burnout and stress. People who look at what they failed to accomplish during the day, not what they did accomplish, and who go to bed and burn themselves out in stress tend to invalidate themselves and others. We need to be encouraging to ourselves as well as our children, and celebrate our own incremental successes as we go through life.

Barrier 5: Using Adultisms

One of the most destructive of all interactive behaviors is what we call *isming*. The suffix *-ism* has a negative connotation in our culture. We tend to tack *-ism*s onto painful problems and/or sicknesses—as in alcoholism, workaholism, and recidivism (the latter means "relapse after improvement"). In this book, *isming* refers to our bad habit of requiring others to read our minds and think as we do.

A *spousism* is committed when one spouse requires another spouse to think, understand, see, and do things exactly as he or she does: "You knew what I wanted. You should have known. If you really cared, I wouldn't have to tell you."

A *supervisorism* occurs when a supervisor holds subordinates accountable for having all the supervisor's expert knowledge: "Surely you realize. . . . You knew what we were expecting."

A *teacherism* happens in the classroom when educators with master's degrees or doctorates assume that students comprehend what they do when they ask, "Why is this important?" (and allow only one right answer).

> To reiterate, an ism is destructive because it requires other people to read our minds. It makes everyone who fails to think, see, and understand exactly as we do feel unacceptable by our standards. Isms ignore the uniqueness of perception and are overtly nonsupportive.

An *adultism* occurs any time an adult forgets what it is like to be a child and then expects, demands, and requires of the child, who has never been an adult, to think, act, understand, see, and do things as an adult. These unrealistic expectations from adults produce impotence, frustration, hostility, and aggression in young people. They undercut the value of expressions of love. They destroy children's belief in their own capabilities, their sense of their own significance, and their influence over events. Still, many of us commit adultisms with our children many times a day.

The language of adultisms is "Why can't you ever? How come you never? Surely you realize! How many times do I have to tell you? Why are you so childish? When will you ever grow up? Did you? Can you? Will you? Won't you? Are you? Aren't you?"

The habitual use of adultisms begins like this: "Why can't you clean up your room?" This adult has forgotten what it was like to be a child. Steve remembers his room when he was a child. It was the center of his mother's universe, but to him it was only a pit stop on his way to immortality. From that perspective, consider a typical exchange between Steve and his mother during Steve's adolescence:

> *She would say, "Clean your room."*
> *Steve would say, "I did," meaning he passed through it twice without tripping.*
> *She would say, "No, you didn't," meaning she could not eat off the floor. "What will the neighbors think?"*

The child's view and the adult's view were utterly irreconcilable.

Adolescence is a time for self-discovery. It is a very important time, during which the focus is inward. In that context, understanding friendship is much more important than having a tidy bedroom. Finding an identity, discovering oneself, and sorting through feelings are infinitely more critical than getting the laundry done right after school. Given this primary focus, expecting thoughtfulness, consideration, and insight about important issues and events from adolescents involved in self-discovery is inappropriate and quite futile.

If we put forth such demands as "Why can't you ever . . . ? How come you never . . . ? Surely you realize. . . . You'll never learn," we are pounding a lot of unnecessary nails of discouragement into the adolescent's spirit. The result will be a child who believes that questions are tricks adults use to make children expose themselves so the adults can put them down. Children learn that the best possible response to anything we ask is "I don't know." This phrase is the great defense that young people use to repel adultisms.

To reiterate, an ism is destructive because it requires other people to read our minds. It makes everyone who fails to think, see, and understand exactly as we do feel unacceptable by our standards. Isms ignore the uniqueness of perception and are overtly nonsupportive.

Builder 5: Respect

The language of respect is "What was your understanding of . . . ? Let me be sure I understand. Under what circumstances would you need to check with me?"

It is very easy to slip into threatening, correcting, directing, and expecting when we have very little time and lots to do. As an expedient, we threaten, correct, direct, and expect ourselves right through the day. In the process, we lose the chance to affirm and validate our children's experiences through dialogue.

When we can substitute respect for adultisms, when we understand that attitudes and behaviors come from perceptions and beliefs, we give children the chance to internalize experience. Young people cannot gain wisdom as long as they are afraid to have the experience or as long as we analyze it for them. If we keep insisting on our superior knowledge, our children will be inhibited from gathering knowledge. It is destructive to expect them to see what we see rather than exploring what they see and then comparing notes. And if we automatically assault them with "Why can't you ever . . . ? How come you never . . . ?" we squelch their enthusiasm with the possibility that they might disappoint us.

To avoid adultisms, we must respect all five dimensions of perception. To express respect to our spouses, we say, "What was your understanding of what I planned to take with me on this trip?" To express respect in the classroom, we say, "What ideas did you get from this paragraph as you read it?" or "In addition to that, how many of you became aware of this, and what is your understanding of that as I have been explaining it to you?" To express it on the job, we say, "What was your understanding of what we needed to have done on that project?"

Once we use the questions "What?" "Where?" "When?" "How?" "In what way?" and "Under what circumstances?" we have shown respect for the uniqueness of each individual's perception. If we do not show such respect, we deny the most beautiful characteristic of the human race: our diversity. Our uniqueness as individuals is our greatest value, both to ourselves and our society.

PUTTING THEM ALL TOGETHER

DO YOU CREATE ANY OF the barriers regularly with someone you love? Do you believe that if you worked at it you could erect them less often? We are not suggesting that you be perfect. Children will endure adultisms 20 percent of the time when they can say if asked, "Most of the time Dad deals with us firmly, but he always shows us dignity and respect, so if he's asking why we didn't do things his way, he must be having a bad day. Check him out tomorrow." If they heard adultisms most of the time, they would be more likely to say, "Don't fool with Dad on any terms. Most days are likely to be bad with him. Get high, get loaded, get stoned, get out of there, but don't get in his way."

Let's look at some examples as a means of summing up barriers and builders. Suppose four-year-old Linda becomes stuck when her tricycle wheel runs off the sidewalk. There are several ways a parent could handle this situation that would decrease feelings of capability:

• *Directing:* "Don't just sit there and cry. Get off and push the tricycle back on the sidewalk." Directing children through each step instead of exploring how a task can be accomplished sends the message that children are incapable of doing the task on their own without specific directions.

• *Explaining:* "That's what happens when you don't watch where you are going. Get off and push your trike back onto the sidewalk." Explaining what happened and how to fix it, instead of helping children examine and analyze their own problems, is neglecting an opportunity to foster the perception that the children are capable.

• *Rescuing:* "Don't cry, honey. I'll fix it for you." If we rush in and save our children, we are telling them they are incapable of taking care of their lives. By allowing them to take the consequences of their actions, we are telling them they are capable of handling both the behavior and the consequences.

• *Assuming:* "Be sure you don't let your wheel come off the edge of the sidewalk, because your bike will get stuck." This remark reflects a combination of barriers. Assuming that the child would not stay away from the edge of the sidewalk led to a form of directing. And directing involved an attempt to rescue the child in advance. Assuming keeps us from letting the child ride down the sidewalk and discover the problem. These barriers create an extremely frustrating experience for children.

• *Using adultisms:* "You knew you were supposed to keep the handlebars straight. How come you never keep your eyes on the sidewalk? Why can't you ever do it right? Surely you realize what will happen if you don't! When will you ever listen?" Children feel personally attacked by adultisms, because this type of remark implies "Well, I should have known you weren't big enough to ride by yourself yet." In short, by attacking the person and failing to point to the problem instead of exploring the problem, adults make children feel worthless and incapable.

What might be an appropriate response to Linda's predicament, then?

"Whoops! Honey, what do you think would happen if you got off your tricycle and backed it up?" That question may seem very similar to explaining or directing, but there is a subtle and important difference. The final answer must come from Linda after she pauses to consider the question. She may even try out the suggestion to find out what would happen. This would represent fruitful exploration of the experience conducted by the child and encouraged by the parent. Linda's perception of bikes and sidewalks might even change, and the change would constitute true learning.

ATTITUDES

THE KEY COMPONENTS IN ALL of the barriers and builders are attitudes. The attitudes inherent in the barriers are negative and disrespectful. The attitudes inherent in the builders are positive and respectful.

It might be our tone of voice alone that invites children to consider their own capabilities. Our tone of voice changes when we change our attitudes. Consider the following examples.

Scott enjoyed being with his friends more than he enjoyed being home. When he did come home, his mother would say in a sarcastic tone of voice, "Well, it's about time you came home." This remark only confirmed Scott's decision that home was not a pleasant place to be. But when Scott's mother changed her attitude, Scott enjoyed being home more often. The next time Scott came home late, she said, "I'm so glad to see you. I really enjoy having you around." The results were positive because the atmosphere created by the change in attitude was respectful, as reflected in Scott's mother's tone of voice.

In another example, one father in our program told us that his family had been through two treatment programs, three psychiatrists, and two psychologists, and he and his wife had finally given up hope of having a positive relationship with their daughter. But within a week of learning about the barriers and builders, he told us, "We experienced a level of closeness, trust, and communication that I would never have believed possible with that daughter. I discovered that I was putting up all five barriers daily. As soon as I cut down on the frequency of the barriers, even before I learned to use the builders, her responsiveness increased dramatically."

The barriers teach children to be passive and unresponsive. When we command, "Pick that up; put that away; it's time to get in here and get something to eat," we are creating resistance in our children. The builders not only build perceptions of capability, significance, and influence but also—when we remove the five barriers—create a climate of respect in which dialogue is likely to occur.

CHILDREN SEE, CHILDREN DO

ONCE THE BARRIERS ARE PULLED down and the builders are being used, the next step in helping children develop strong perceptions of personal capabilities is structuring situations in which they can recognize and understand appropriate behaviors and role models. Children sharpen their self-evaluation skills when we talk with them about what they admire in people. We can model for them by being articulate and specific in pointing out admirable qualities.

The EIAG comes into play here, too: "What was it you admired in that person? In what way is that an admirable quality for you? How could you show that same kind of characteristic in your own life?" If young people have never identified the capabilities they admire, then how do they internalize them?

> Children sharpen their self-evaluation skills when we talk with them about what they admire in people. We can model for them by being articulate and specific in pointing out admirable qualities.

Chimpanzees and gorillas copy each other automatically, but human beings, if encouraged to do so, can look at people they encounter and thoughtfully decide whether they want to copy them. It is only young people with no sense of their own capabilities who imitate others automatically without going through the judging process. Reading fiction and talking about the characters are fruitful ways of exploring these questions.

The Japanese endlessly study the lives of successful people, not to copy them but to learn the principles that made them successful so they can fit these principles into their own lives. In so doing, they are pursuing this judging activity, sharpening their powers of discernment, and learning what it is they respect.

THE INFLUENCE OF MEDIA MODELS

THE MEDIA HAS A TREMENDOUS impact on children today. Up to the age of eighteen, children spend an average of eighteen thousand hours watching television. During that time, they see an average of 180,000 minutes of commercials, which teach them that self-medication and instant gratification are desirable, that warmth and closeness are easily obtainable through using the right product or services, and that the greatest success our sports heroes and other celebrities can aspire to involves hustling beverages and products. As parents, we need to compensate for these destructive messages by helping children think critically about what they see and by modeling, in our relationships with them, the things we value.

When we assume, rescue, direct, expect, and use adultisms, we are modeling a lack of belief in the capabilities of our children. The children react by being defensive, distant, and unresponsive. The common dictum "Do as I say, not as I do" does not inspire their trust and admiration. In fact, children are likely to do as you do—or, to go to the other extreme, do the opposite of what you do. The critical lesson is that we must serve as positive models for our children, offering ourselves without demanding their attention.

It is important to mention that although modeling is central to parenting, your children have the potential to learn what you do not know and do what you have not been able to do. It is critically important to inspire self-confidence in this generation of young people, who must go into a world characterized by continual discoveries. Those equipped to learn how to find their own way will be the most successful. The highest goal to which a parent or teacher can aspire is to raise their children or teach their students to be more capable than they themselves are or ever were.

5

Fostering Perceptions of Personal Significance

T HE SECOND OF the Significant Seven relates to the greatest need at the core of human existence. This is a dual need: to find meaning in life and to perceive and experience personal significance.

THE NEED TO BE NEEDED

THE NEED TO BE NEEDED is often more powerful than the need to survive. Human beings are the only species that can be motivated to commit suicide by a perception that their life has no meaning, purpose, or significance. Pioneering psychologist Alfred Adler found that when human beings feel no sense of belonging or importance, they behave in ways that provide them with a false sense of significance. For example, they might seek to compensate by demanding undue attention, using power unproductively, or going after revenge for perceived wrongs. When such an approach fails, they may simply give up. The fact that these patterns of behavior in no way result in an authentic sense of significance makes them no less common. Particularly in young people we find truly extreme behavior—outright rebellion or passive resignation—directly linked to these feelings. These patterns can result in self-destructive behaviors. For example, the sense of insignificance in young people can take the form of drug and alcohol abuse, vandalism, and teenage pregnancy.

Resignation is frequently expressed as anorexia or suicide—overt manifestations of depression, illness, and the lack of a will to live.

Even small babies crave personal meaning. Studies have shown that babies and children placed in orphanages where adults supervise them in groups and do everything for them are frequently developmentally delayed, have health problems, and suffer elevated death rates. In these studies the oversupervised children were compared with others who experienced virtually identical settings, with one major difference. In the latter case, the staff was trained to spend time daily with each child one on one. A staff person engaged in dialogue with each child and invited each child to assist in significant tasks and activities. These children, in direct contrast to the first group, show accelerated development, lower than normal frequencies of health problems, and reduced mortality rates.

Recent studies into the chemistry of the brain reinforce the assertion that personal significance is a fundamental need. These show that many of the critical brain chemicals that regulate mood, motivation, concentration, feelings, resistance to illness, and depression are highly influenced by perceptions of personal significance. Thus, not only psychological but also physiological evidence points us to this critical ingredient in our overall well-being.

Lest we imply otherwise, it is important to note that all people, not just the young, suffer when they feel themselves to be insignificant. At the other end of the spectrum, among the elderly, the problem is as acute as for the young. Modern medical technology and improved diet have increased the average life expectancy of human beings by thirty years. If you recall our earlier description of the rural/urban revolution, you will realize that while we were increasing the life span, we were simultaneously eliminating many of the roles older people played in our communities. Nowadays, the aged too often do not have a consulting role in the parenting process or on-the-job training for the next generation—critical roles, indeed, for them prior to World War II. As a result of the loss of personal affirmation experienced with the disappearance of our social networks, many older people now suffer depression, disillusionment, despair, premature senility, and even an early death.

The loss of personal meaning, then, can be profound, yet the remedy need not be complex. Research has shown that, as a group, older people who have pets or plants can live several years longer than those with no such pets or plants. Very frequently, when the pets or plants die, so do their owners.

THE POWER OF BEING NEEDED

IN THE CAREGIVING PROFESSIONS, THE profound power of personal significance has long been understood. In previous generations, doctors, nurses, and clergy went through epidemics, violated every rule of contagion, worked to the point of exhaustion, and in most cases still did not fall ill—all because they knew that the lives of others depended on their continued health.

On the patient side, too, recent research shows that people who view themselves as important, unique, and necessary to their work or families are significantly less vulnerable to cancer, strokes, heart attacks, hypertension, and other diseases. Similarly, this perception increases the probability of recovering in people who do become ill. Thus, even at this most basic level—involving our bodily resistance to disease and our motivation to live—the need to believe that we play a contributing role in the lives of people who matter to us has a profoundly positive effect.

> The need to believe that we play a contributing role in the lives of people who matter to us has a profoundly positive effect.

DRUDGERY VERSUS UNIQUE CONTRIBUTIONS

IN CHAPTER 2, WE SHOWED THAT most parents no longer need their children in practical ways to accomplish their daily work. In such a world, the process of developing perceptions of significance in our children is greatly complicated. The barrier behaviors discussed in chapter 4 are particularly relevant in this context, for their effect is to reduce perceptions of personal significance.

The builders, on the other hand, enhance perceptions of personal significance. We have seen that when adults direct young people, they make everything a *chore.* But when adults invite the assistance of young people, they give them a chance to make a meaningful *contribution* to the household.

This distinction is not always easy to discern. Simply loading children down with chores can make them feel as insignificant and frustrated as Cinderella in the classic fairytale. The crucial point is to enable people to feel that their particular contributions are valuable, not simply the drudgery of drones. When the prince decided that he needed Cinderella, the girl's depression and despair—which stemmed from a perception that she was not valued for herself—disappeared.

Regarding chores, as with most situations, one key to helping children feel significant is to involve them in the process of brainstorming and problem solving. Children can help make a list of all the chores that need to be done to help the family run more smoothly. They can then brainstorm for creative ways to accomplish these tasks. Not only to children feel more significant when they are involved; they are more enthusiastic about following plans they have helped create.

DEVELOPING A SENSE OF MEANING AND PURPOSE

TODAY, WITH RITUALS, TRADITIONS, AND family structure more blurred than ever before, it is imperative that we help our young people engage in life-affirming experiences. The key is to guide young people into activities that develop their sense of meaning and purpose. For example, research shows that in cross-age tutoring—in which older young people teach younger people—the tutors profit even more than the tutorees. Why? Because they feel needed. Analogously, peer counselors come away with more than their counselees—because they feel needed. This also works with delinquent young people. When recruited into programs to work with and do things for younger people, they tend to shed much of their delinquent behavior as they come to perceive themselves as needed and significant. Nowhere is this principle clearer than in Alcoholics Anonymous and similar groups. *When people are needed as contributors, they bond, invest, grow, and get healthy. When everything is done for them, they continue to perceive themselves as inadequate and insignificant.*

Families that devote any regular time at all—as little as thirty minutes a week with small children or thirty minutes a month with older children—to some regularly structured ritual, tradition, or activity, have children who experience much less serious difficulty than identical families in the same neighborhoods who spend no time together.

The axiom is simple: When the helpless become the helpers, they gain the sense of dignity and self-respect that is the hallmark of productive well-being. Remember the barrier of doing too much for children? When we do too much, we may make them feel helpless and rob them of the opportunity to maintain their dignity and self-respect.

Helen Duarte-Medina, a teacher in Los Angeles, California, found while working with gang members that when she created a community in the classroom in which young people felt significant, the gangs had less influence on their lives. During an interview, Helen was asked, "Does this help them give up their gangs?" Helen replied, "Oh no, I would not ask them to do that. For many, gangs are their *familia* (family). What I do is help them to find constructive alternatives to gangs and ways to create healthier rituals and traditions within their gangs."

RITUALS AND TRADITIONS

ONCE UPON A TIME, MOST families worked together to perform the work essential for survival. In short, they needed each other. Today, family members frequently go in so many different directions they hardly see each other. And even when they are in the house together, they are often intimate strangers, pursuing divergent interests under one roof.

The shame of it is that meeting the need for personal meaning is so simple. Families that devote any regular time at all—as little as thirty minutes a week with small children or thirty minutes a month with older children—to some regularly structured ritual, tradition, or activity, have children who experience much less serious difficulty than identical families in the same neighborhoods who spend no time together. Research from many sources has shown that children who perceive themselves as important, contributing parts of a functioning set of ongoing relationships *before the age of twelve* are more resistant to peer groups, cults, and extraneous programming during their teenage years than children who perceive themselves as insignificant to others. On the other hand, recent research has shown that when family connection is lacking, children are engaging in sex, drugs, and gang activities at younger and younger ages.

It is true that we no longer have to interact for our survival. Therefore, we must make the effort to structure meaningful activities designed to build close relationships. We need to purposefully create a climate of support in our families where young people can develop the perceptions and skills necessary for successful living. One effective ritual that fosters just such growth—and provides the chance for creating other rituals—is the family meeting.

Family Meetings. There are a number of specific ways in which participation in the family meeting process builds strong perceptions of meaning, purpose, and significance:

1. Meetings enable families to practice dialogue.

2. Children learn the important life skills of brainstorming and problem solving.

3. Children can experience significance through meaningful involvement.

4. Meetings become an important ritual and tradition when they are kept regular and predictable, preferably occurring at least once a week. (Many families take the phone off the hook during their family meetings and ask friends not to call during that time, thus reinforcing the notion that the meetings are of primary importance.)

5. Successful people are "good finders." Meetings afford practice in verbalizing positive feedback in the form of compliments and acknowledgments of work well done.

6. Giving young people the chance to chair family meetings (occasionally, in rotation with others) is a good way to foster their perceptions of their own significance.

Spiritual Affirmation. Family meetings, which will be discussed in more detail in chapter 6, afford children many practical opportunities to feel important. However, human beings are spiritual as well as practical creatures. By "spiritual," we don't necessarily mean "religious." We define *spirituality* as an active identification with things greater than one's self that give life meaning and purpose. In this context, friendship, trust, loyalty, affirmation, and respect are spiritual values. Thus, when we affirm people's significance, we reinforce their spiritual qualities as well. Spiritual affirmation stems from self-affirmation.

THE ART OF AFFIRMATION

JOHN NAISBETT, IN HIS BEST-SELLING book *Megatrends,* raised the issue of high-tech versus high-touch, indicating that as our lifestyle has become saturated with high technology, we have begun to experience deficits in what he calls "high-touch," or personal contact and affirmation. He went on to explore the role of quality circles and other vehicles used in business settings to help people feel listened to, taken seriously, and significant. In the terms we have used in this book, we might paraphrase his remarks by saying that as we

THREE CONDITIONS FOR SPIRITUAL AFFIRMATION

Three conditions are necessary for spiritual affirmation:

1. To be listened to—not just heard but understood
2. To be taken seriously—not just understood but accepted, loved, and respected
3. To feel genuinely needed for one's own personal worth, contributions, and significance

effected our rural/urban revolution, we began to allow the dialogue and collaboration that kept us in touch with each other to disappear. Thus, not only did most relationship systems become more stressful, but our opportunities to affirm each other's significance diminished greatly.

Remember that the second principle in the Significant Seven is to develop a sense of personal significance in children. Given the effects of our rural/urban revolution—the diminishment of high-touch—we need to relearn and put into practice the high-touch techniques we have lost. Chief among them is dialogue.

Dialogue

Dialogue is a meaningful exchange of perceptions in a nonthreatening climate of support and genuine interest. Without engaging in genuine dialogue with people of importance to them, our young people find it difficult to perceive themselves as meaningful and significant. Yet, dialogue is surfacing in research as the foundation of critical thinking, moral and ethical development, judgmental maturity, bonding, closeness, and trust.

The EIAG process described earlier is useful in initiating dialogue with young people, but only where the urge to explore their perceptions and to encourage them to discover new perceptions about a situation is genuine. A re-

quirement, then, for initiating dialogue is an attitude on the adult's part of genuine interest, devoid of the need to manipulate the direction or conclusions of the discussion.

As our earlier discussion of EIAG suggested, our attitudes show through even when we are unaware of them. Consider this example:

> *A mother in one of our programs was working on improving her attitude toward her son. She decided to convey to him the fact that he was important to her. When he came into the room to talk with her, she reached over and turned the radio off. He stopped talking, looked at her in amazement, and said, "Why did you do that?"*
>
> *She answered, "Well, I just wanted to hear what you had to say."*
>
> *He retorted, "Is that something you learned in your workshop?"*
>
> *"As a matter of fact, it is," she answered. "I learned that since you are important to me, I should take the steps to pay full attention to what you have to say."*
>
> *"You don't need to do that," he said.*

Given the effects of our rural/urban revolution—the diminishment of high-touch—we need to relearn and put into practice the high-touch techniques we have lost. Chief among them is dialogue.

She wondered whether her approach was working. In our workshop we had explained that most human beings are a little embarrassed when they receive unexpected attention. When we asked later how her son had responded next, she told us, "He went ahead and told me what he was going to say, and he beamed a little bit."

We queried her some more. "Even though he told you that you didn't have to do that, did he go back and turn the radio on?"

She said, "No."

"Did he go ahead and share with you?"

"Yes."

"Did you hear him a little more clearly than usual?"

"Yes."

"Did you achieve your goal of showing him that he was significant?"

"Yes."

Though this mother's attempts seem a little abrupt and awkward, it was her attitude that led to a successful dialogue, and that is the point of the story. Our attitudes are determined by what we believe about the people we are talking with and how we ask them the EIAG questions. If we deliver the questions as if we were conducting an interrogation, we will evoke resistance. If we use them to manipulate—to prove a preconceived point—we can evoke hostility and even silence. But if we are truly open to dialogue and are truly curious about our children's thoughts and feelings, even if we are awkward in initiating it, productive communication will be the result.

However, even when our attitude is one of respect and genuine interest, it is possible that our children will not perceive it that way. As was true for the boy in the prior story, our children may be baffled initially by changes in our attitudes. They may continue to react in accordance with our former behavior. We may need to give them time to adjust to a shift in perceptions, and this will require patience on our part.

Also, like the rest of us, adolescents are easily embarrassed when trying to deal with their inner needs and feelings, and they may respond awkwardly when we try to initiate an affirming dialogue. They might even feel confused by needing our affirmation at the same time they are trying to show their independence. They can feel encouraged by our concern and, simultaneously, discouraged by our efforts to evoke their responses. Thus, we must proceed carefully, understanding that open dialogue can at first seem threatening to adolescents even while we are certain of its benefits. And what is the teenager's predictable response when he or she is backed into a corner by words? You know it; be ready for it—that old stand-by: "I don't know."

The Safety of "I Don't Know"

In an earlier chapter, we explained why kids say "I don't know." Usually it is because they learn very early in life that adults use questions to get kids to expose themselves so the adults can attack them. In that context, the safest response to any adult question is "I don't know."

In the course of this book, we have identified many factors in today's world that inhibit dialogue and thus reduce our chance of affirming the worth of our youth. One such factor that deserves highlighting is the content-oriented, rote-and-recall model of education that has pervaded our system of education. (Many people call this approach to learning Skinnerian learning, although B. F. Skinner moved steadily over his career toward a more perceptually and transactionally based model for working with human beings.) Combine this unimaginative pedagogical approach with the sensitivity to attitude and fear of exposure of most adolescents, and you have an environment in which dialogue dies on the lips.

In 1986, the National Assessment Project, established by the U.S. Congress to monitor America's school improvement effort, presented data indicating that after the sixth grade, American children show no significant changes in the areas of critical thinking, judgmental maturity, and the emergence of moral and ethical capabilities. Whatever skills children show in these areas in the twelfth grade were those they attained by the sixth, even though the children had the developmental potential to go well beyond this level. Researchers traced much of this retarded development to the overuse of objective tests at the secondary level. Objective tests are easier to grade and handle than, say, essay exams. So the schools' need for efficiency outweighed the students' needs for more interaction, dialogue, and collaboration with their teachers, case studies, and essay exams—in short, more challenges in school.

Researchers also found that secondary teachers had a strong tendency to grade or correct grammar but to avoid significant dialogue about the organization, implications, alternatives, thoughts, ideas, and structure of student papers.

This tendency, too, worked directly against the developmental needs of the age group in question.

As children pass the developmental age of eight, they move into a zone in which thought, volition, insight, and understanding begin to take over from rote and recall in their learning. However, to take this leap in reasoning, children must engage in dialogue and collaborative experiences with more mature people. It is just these types of experiences that our school system as well as our own altered family life has been keeping from our children.

> What we really need to teach ourselves and each other is the language of love.

As a result of these social and educational patterns, young people (and many adults) are afraid to think and explore at all, for they have been taught that they will be penalized if they say the wrong thing. And because the current system of education demands conformity, those teachers who sincerely want to encourage their students to think and explore are blocked in their efforts by the children themselves. For at the age of six or seven, children learn that it is not safe to offer original thought or dialogue but is only safe to guess at and deliver the answer the teacher wants or, failing that, to offer up "I don't know."

One teacher who attended our leadership training workshop expressed the problem poignantly:

> *For the last nineteen years as a teacher, I have been rendering children impotent in my classroom with my teaching methods and then criticizing them for their lack of initiative. But the chickens came home to roost last night. My daughter was to answer several questions for her math homework. One of the questions was "Which of the following charts do you like best and why?" The next question was "Which of the following charts do you like least and why?" The third question was "Which did you find easiest to understand and why?" My daughter was desperate, because she had not compared notes with the other kids to find out which one the teacher wanted them to pick. I explained that these were questions inviting her to make her own choice and to justify it. She said, "You don't understand this teacher. If I pick the one she doesn't want, I'll get a bad grade. And I really need to do well in this class." I argued with her for a while, and she*

finally—grudgingly—took out a sheet of paper and answered the questions as she saw them. In the morning I found that paper in the trash. She was off early to second-guess the teacher with the other kids.

This child had learned that one of the riskiest things she could do was to offer a personal opinion. It was far easier to give the teacher what she wanted than to take the risk of doing some thinking on her own.

Adultisms Versus Understanding

We have a whole population of parents attending workshops on family stress, intimacy, communication, and parenting skills. These diligent workshop participants then go home and paint themselves into a corner with those familiar old adultisms: "Did you? Can you? Will you? Won't you? Are you? Aren't you? Why can't you ever? How come you never? Surely you realize! How many times do I have to tell you?" What we really need to teach ourselves and each other is the language of love.

The two fundamental phrases in this special language, phrases that show a genuine interest in the other's response, are "What was your understanding of what happened?" and "Let me be sure I understand what you understand." You recognize the other basic phrases in the language of love: "What?" "Where?" "When?" and "How?" These questions, used not to interrogate but to genuinely invite the other person to share or explore experiences and meaning, are the means of achieving dialogue. The key, again, is attitude. If by our attitude we convey the message "I am completely open to your point of view," then slowly the person's resistance, both natural and learned, will give way to the kind of dialogue that will celebrate their openness and affirm their importance as human beings.

Friendship, Love—and Dialogue

One more benefit accrues from the meaningful exchange of perceptions within the context of genuine acceptance: friendship.

When we are in love, what constitutes our courtship behavior? How do we attempt to gain our lover's affection? We spend hours and hours in dialogue, act interested, and create something beautiful called love. Then, if we are not

THREE PERCEPTIONS NECESSARY FOR CLOSENESS AND TRUST

Three perceptions are necessary before closeness and trust can be established in a relationship:

1. This person is listening to me.
2. I can risk my perceptions and feelings here without being discounted for them.
3. This person's behavior toward me indicates that what I think or have to offer is significant.

Without these three perceptions, we cannot trust others, cannot believe what they say, and must hide from them.

careful, we cut out the dialogue, substitute expectations, begin the business of marriage together, and ruin the relationship. If we ever want to rebuild the marriage, we must go back to dialogue.

If you tell me you love me but fail to listen to me, discount my perceptions and feelings, and make the mistake of doing everything for me so that I feel totally useless around you, I will resent you for saying you love me. However, if you listen to me, treat my perceptions and feelings with respect, and affirm my contributions to the relationship, I will know you respect me and care deeply in your own way, even if you never tell me you love me. I will know that in your eyes I am worth something.

What is the state of affection within our American families? In general, we have developed a very lazy, unproductive pattern of dealing with each other within the home. Count the number of times this week you have found yourself, in allegedly intimate relationships that are important to you, dealing with those you love this way: "Did you? Can you? Do you? Will you? Won't you? Are you? Aren't you?" These questions can all be responded to with a harumph, a shrug, a grunt, or stony silence.

"Did you have a good day?" "I guess so." "Did that work out all right?" "I guess so." "Is everything all right?" "I guess so."

This is the language of disrespect, not love. It says, "I am going to reduce you to a multiple-choice animal. You can pick options I have chosen, but I am not going to invest much time into finding out anything much about your life."

We can bring back dialogue—and bring back love. The first step is to stop creating the barriers and using the multiple-choice/true-or-false language of disrespect. The second is to start using the language of respect through the EIAG process. And the third step is to be patient while children get used to the new climate that these changes will create.

> Generic praise never affirms the significance of others' work; specific recognition always does. This means taking the time to recognize what it was that a child did well.

THE BARRIER OF A THREATENING ATMOSPHERE

CONDITIONAL LOVE, APPROVAL, AND ACCEPTANCE create a threatening atmosphere that prohibits dialogue and the free flow of affection.

> *Whenever a person perceives threat in any environment, including the real or imagined loss of regard, the possibility of rejection, or the possibility of feeling foolish, he or she will stop learning and practice self-defense. He or she will lie, scapegoat, cheat, or do anything that keeps the threatening person from seeing him or her as he or she is.*
>
> *—Kurt Lewin*

> *Until I can risk appearing imperfect in your eyes, without fear that it will cost me something, I can't really learn from you.*
>
> *—Rudolph Dreikurs*

Lewin and Dreikurs were aware of the habits that frequently interfere with our ability to help our children and others feel significant and acceptable to us. Here are three specific behaviors that create the kind of threatening atmosphere they refer to:

1. Substituting grades for our children's identity ("You are an A student, and your brother is a C student")

2. Rewarding love or withholding love based on performance
3. Giving generic praise and approval rather than specific feedback

Generic praise never affirms the significance of others' work; specific recognition always does. This means taking the time to recognize what it was that a child did well.

The language of specific recognition is this: "I feel . . . about . . . because . . ." For example: "I feel pleased about having the kitchen cleaned because it is nicer to cook in a clean kitchen," or "I feel upset that the kitchen is not cleaned up because it is very unpleasant to cook in a messy kitchen." Such responses not only give clear feedback but also are more trustworthy than general remarks. Compare the paper marked "great" with the one that comes back marked, "I really like the way your paragraphs were organized." Such specific feedback constitutes true affirmation by drawing attention to the writer's own particular capabilities.

Many people believe that if we say *good* things and give others lots of praise, they will do better. In reality, they may become more fearful, dependent, and vulnerable.

The problem with praise is that it is effective in making people dependent on the approval or opinion of others. Praise encourages an outer locus of control.

THE PRESSURE TO PERFORM

CHILDREN WHO COME TO BELIEVE that our love, praise, or affection is contingent on their pleasing us and doing what we want them to do become the most vulnerable of all people. For when they are unable to deliver, they grow desperate to keep our love.

Recently, we found that a significant majority of teachers and parents use ineffective management strategies with children. These strategies consist of detailed criticism for failure and unspecific, general praise for success. Personal criticism and generic praise teach young people to work for approval rather than insight and understanding and to view errors as a reflection of diminishing personal worth. Many teachers have been trained to draw round smiley faces, offer A plusses, and scribble vacuous comments such as "terrific" on school papers. These strategies are counterproductive. They have, at best, the capacity to raise people to mediocrity because they provide no specific feedback or insight to support growth and maturation.

To help children grow and gain the tools they need to succeed in life, we must tell them specifically what they did well. Our feedback should convey the exact standards against which we judge their work. In addition, we must convey to them that we actually understood what they did. Here is an example of constructive feedback:

> *One thing that makes this paper effective is its well-documented footnotes. I have underscored a couple that I think you could use as a model for next time. I also notice that your thesis statement is clear and outlines the rest of your paper clearly. I've underlined a couple of sentences that I thought were particularly effective.*

These comments give the student specifics against which to compare points in the next paper. They also prepare the student for college, where professors won't give smiley faces but will demand performance.

The tendency in our culture to be specific in our criticism but vague in our approval has taught young people to downgrade approval but to wait nervously for the "but" that is the usual prelude to criticism. They quickly come to believe that their ultimate goal is to avoid criticism and attain approval.

Regarding the common tendency among parents to confuse their children with their grades, an antidote might be a comment such as this: "Son, I'm unhappy with the way your report card came out. I don't believe it reflects the kind of effort you could have put in. I'm very interested to know what you believe produced the report card as you have it now and what you believe it will take to change that in the next semester." Not only do these remarks distinguish the child from the grades, but they give specific feedback and explore the child's perceptions by offering him the opportunity to explain the situation and consider ways to correct it.

"What is your understanding of what happened?" "What is your understanding of why this is an important issue for us?" "Since this has come up, I need to know what you intend to do, or are willing to do, to correct the situation." Such comments invite the child to collaborate and to contribute an interpretation and solution. The effect is to foster development of an inner locus of control.

MORE THAN WORDS

IN THIS CHAPTER, WE HAVE established the critical need to affirm our children's sense of personal significance through increased and enhanced dialogue. But it is important to make clear that dialogue is not limited to communication through words alone. Dialogue takes place when there is a meaningful exchange of perceptions in a climate of support, safety, and understanding. You can communicate a lot with a nod or even with well-timed silence.

Every day we say to our peers, "You seem a little down. Is everything OK?" We are letting them know that they are communicating to us with their posture and their attitudes. We need to make sure we do the same with our children.

> Once we bring the collaborative experience of dialogue back into our households—by reinstituting meaningful roles, family rituals, and traditions—our young people will thrive on the affirmation within the family and come naturally to perceive themselves as having purposeful, significant lives.

Dialogue can take myriad forms if we remain open to the possibilities. For example, we foster dialogue when we stop asking close-ended questions (questions that lend themselves to yes or no responses) such as "Did you have a good day?" and ask instead, "What things happened to you today?" If we do ask, "How was your day?" and the reply is "OK," we can show that we really care by asking, "What was the most OK thing that happened?" or "What does 'OK' mean?"

If dialogue seems to be inhibited because our children refuse to participate, we might need to ask ourselves what we are doing to create resistance. It's true that we may not be creating resistance but may be insensitive to the dialogue styles of our children. Some people like to talk a lot, and some people are naturally quiet. Some people are simply slower to respond than others, requiring that we be patient. Perhaps we need to tune in to nonverbal cues and body language when our efforts at dialogue with our children are bogging down.

Once we bring the collaborative experience of dialogue back into our households—by reinstituting meaningful roles, family rituals, and traditions—our young people will thrive on the affirmation within the family and come naturally to perceive themselves as having purposeful, significant lives.

6

Fostering Perceptions of Personal Influence over One's Life

THE THIRD PRINCIPLE in the Significant Seven involves the individual's perception that personal thoughts, choices, and actions actually affect the events and circumstances of his or her life. One characteristic of people who tend to get into trouble is their perception that they have little or no power to affect what they experience in life. They put their faith in fate or luck and are frequently impotent in the face of choices. In clinical terms, such people are described as having an external locus of control or a victim mentality. They are passive victims of outside events.

Such people usually take one of three paths through life: (1) they continually feel depressed at their failure in finding success and happiness outside themselves; (2) they run on a treadmill all their lives while harboring the hope that someday they will find fulfillment out there; or (3) they live a life of rebellion, seeking a false sense of power.

In contrast, people with a strong sense of influence over events are said to have a predominately internal locus of control or personal responsibility. Their experiences and behavior frequently reflect their internal decisions and choices.

AN EXTERNAL LOCUS OF CONTROL

A PERSON WITH AN EXTERNAL locus of control subscribes to the following description of reality: "It doesn't matter much what people do. Things either work out or they don't. What happens is simply a matter of good or bad luck. I have no control over what happens to me. People do things to me that I don't necessarily deserve, but that is simply the way life works."

In perceiving power to lie outside themselves, not within, these people are highly susceptible to others' opinions regarding their own self-worth and potential actions. Young people with this point of view are particularly vulnerable to peer pressure. They are likely to become pleasers and approval junkies and to become depressed when they do not live up to the expectations others hold of them. Their happiness depends solely on factors external to themselves—such as material possessions, success as defined by others, and the love of others. Many people with an external locus of control are competitive, feeling that the only way to gain approval is to win over others. It is not uncommon for them to criticize and insult habitually. Rudolph Dreikurs called this "deflating another in the hope of inflating oneself in comparison."

AN INTERNAL LOCUS OF CONTROL

PEOPLE WITH AN INTERNAL LOCUS of control have the following perceptions of themselves: "While I cannot always control what happens to me, I can usually influence how I deal with things events that happen in my life." "What I experience is largely a result of the decisions I make and the effort I put forth. I believe I can usually find a way to work out problems or improve relationships, often by talking to people. I believe that a correlation exists between what I do and what I experience, between the effort I put forth and the rewards I reap from life. And when I can't influence what happens, I can still decide how I will let circumstances affect me."

People with an internal locus of control may enjoy material possessions and the approval of others, but they don't depend on them for their happiness. Rather, their happiness emanates from within themselves. It is an expression of their gratitude for the miracles of life, peace of mind, compassion, and love for others. They feel successful, believe their success comes from inside themselves, and bring that feeling to everything they do.

On his cassette tape series, *Choosing Your Own Greatness,* Dr. Wayne Dyer tells a delightful story: One day an old alley cat in his wanderings saw an interesting sight. A young alley cat was running around and around trying to catch its own tail. He watched in fascination for a long time. When the young alley cat finally stopped to catch his breath, the old alley cat asked, "Would you mind telling me what you are doing?"

The young alley cat said, "Certainly. I went to Cat Philosophy School and learned that happiness is in our tails. I am going to keep chasing my tail because someday I will catch it and get a big bite of happiness."

The old alley cat said, "Well, I have never been to Cat Philosophy School, but I know it is true that happiness is in our tails. However, I have found that when I just wander around enjoying life, it follows me everywhere I go."

This story is not meant to imply that people with an internal locus of control simply wander around enjoying life. Rather, they actively bring a sense of potency and determination to whatever they do. Thus, they make successful decisions and take effective actions that bring them joy.

> People with an internal locus of control may enjoy material possessions and the approval of others, but they don't depend on them for their happiness. Rather, their happiness emanates from within themselves.

EXTERNAL CONDITIONS
AND LOCUS OF CONTROL

THE FACT THAT A NUCLEAR bomb may explode at any moment gives many people an excuse to say, "I can't do anything to change things—I give up." But every generation has faced its own imminent mortality, and in days gone by the threat was often a lot closer to home. In primitive times there was never certainty that the men would return home from the hunt. Pioneers, Indians, and the environment were constantly destroying each other. In bygone days, any of a wide range of diseases could swiftly destroy whole communities.

Today, many of us live in relative health and safety, but other threats lurk close to home. Drugs such as tranquilizers and alcohol constantly challenge our perception of control. The message inherent in these drugs is "Why use your own resources to solve problems? Just dull your senses so the problem won't bother you so much." Our children, whose locus of control is not yet firmly established within, are particularly vulnerable to such threats, which often take the form of temptations. If we are not careful, and if we erect the barriers discussed in earlier chapters, we will reinforce the perception in our children that "there is nothing we can do." By doing so, we will raise outer-directed children adrift on a sea of random influences.

MODELING

THE ALTERNATIVE IS TO MODEL behavior directed by a strong locus of control within ourselves. This requires scrupulous self-examination and rigorous self-control. If, for example, we come home from work and blame others for every difficult situation we have encountered throughout the day, we are giving in to the temptation to pass control of our lives to external factors—and teaching our children to do so by example. A more positive, less passive approach to a hard day at work is reflected in this remark: "A difficult situation has arisen at work, and I haven't decided what I am going to do about it yet."

In another example, a mother who comes to us and says, "Do something with my child," has no hope of improving her relationship with her daughter, because she perceives herself as powerless, and as such she is modeling passive behavior. Our job becomes helping her change her beliefs so she can say, "Help me learn what to do differently with this child." When she can frame her problem this way, she will have accepted the perception that her locus of control lies within herself and will then be more likely to find a solution.

HELPING CHILDREN FEEL EFFECTIVE!

HOW DO YOUNG PEOPLE DEVELOP perceptions of themselves as effective or ineffective (often called "winners" or "losers")? The original influences that foster "loser" perceptions are these parental practices: threatening, correcting, directing, assuming, and expecting well beyond the capacity of the child. The direct result of such child-rearing practices is the belief, on the child's part, that "I am a helpless pawn and what I experience in life has little to do with my actions choices and wishes."

The Boob Tube Strikes Again

The external locus of control reflected in such a statement is reinforced by television, which continuously portrays the five themes discussed in chapter 2. Together, these themes convey the notion that life is a matter of fate, luck, magic, and instant gratification and that even the most complex mess in human life can have a happy ending—or at least be easily resolved during the span of a commercial or a single program. Television often reinforces magical thinking that encourages children to believe that solutions are instantaneous and easy, that results are obtainable through some external product or service, and that drinking and casual sex are the primary social activities.

There are indications that the more television people watch, the more pessimistic they become about life. The result in young people is often seen as a decline in their tolerance for frustrating situations and the notion of persevering through them until they work things out. Many get married, for instance, with the perception that if they are not happy immediately, they should simply give up and move on. Family counselors are reporting great resistance among younger clients to the notion that some unhappiness is inevitable when two individuals share a life.

The latest brain research has shown that the brain does not develop properly when young children watch too much television. Many believe television and video games are influential in creating violent tendencies in children.

Most of us have experienced how addictive it can be to channel surf, even when it is impossible to find anything worth watching. All of this takes time away from building close relationships and learning valuable life skills.

Meaning What You Say

In addition to those barrier behaviors discussed earlier, several common parental practices go into the making of losers. The first is the wielding of false threats—for example, "You're grounded forever." (We haven't yet found any parents who are willing to cancel all their plans to follow through and supervise their grounded children forever.) The second is the self-inflicted and phony threat—for example, "If you do that, I'll just die." Parents who promise their children that they will just die ought to keep their promises and drop dead. Then their children will know that they mean what they say.

Strictness and Permissiveness

In the perennial argument between strictness and permissiveness, both sides miss the point. Strictness is excessive manipulation or control by adults. It often causes those controlled to feel powerless and frustrated. Children who do not believe that they have influence over their environment and their destinies often seek power in destructive ways. Excessive strictness usually trains young people to give in or rebel.

Parental permissiveness, on the other hand, usually produces insecurity and the belief that there is very little cause and effect in life. Permissiveness trains young people to use their resources to manipulate other people into their service. The midpoint between these two extremes, and the arena in which children can feel safe while learning to exert their own power, is reached through the gentle, firm, and consistent process of setting reasonable limits on behavior within the context of family life.

Setting Limits

We can see the value of limits best by observing what happens when they are not set. Many parents pamper their children in the name of love. In truth, pampering is one of the most unloving things we can do to our children.

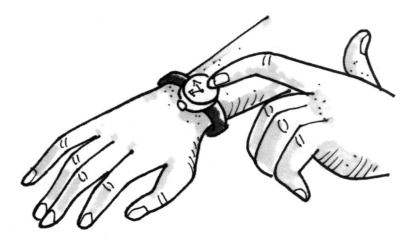

When things come too easily for children, they grow up thinking that the world owes them. When we give in to our children, we are teaching them to put all their intelligence and energy into learning how to manipulate others into taking care of them, instead of learning to take care of themselves. It is the opposite of love to let them off the hook so they do not have to experience agreed-on consequences. Children need limits precisely to learn consequences. But they need realistic limits.

Too often, we set unreasonable limits with our children, because we wait until after something has gone wrong to decide what we'll do about it. When we have failed to anticipate the likely consequences of a situation, we often react with anger and say such meaningless things as "You'll never go out again as long as you live if you are late again."

Setting limits is an exercise in using our wisdom and experience to anticipate possible problems and solve them in advance. Determining a curfew hour together with the child offers a good opportunity for establishing limits in such a way that the child's sense of control remains intact and reinforced. Consider the following conversation:

> S etting limits is an exercise in using our wisdom and experience to anticipate possible problems and solve them in advance.

"Honey, is there any possible reason why you might be delayed tonight?"
"No, I don't believe there is."

"Then, I'll expect you to be home on time. If something happens to prevent you from coming home on time, I expect you to call immediately. If you don't call but decide to come home late, I'm going to require you to stay home all next week so you will come to understand that the privilege of going out is based on the responsibility of coming home on time."

If, after these conditions are made clear, the child chooses to come home later than the agreed-on time, it is not necessary or effective to get angry. Friendly firmness, dignity, and respect are more effective: "Honey, I'm sorry you decided to handle it this way, but I've got to respect your decision to stay home for the rest of the week." The child may act confused and object: "I don't understand. What do you mean, 'my decision'?" "Well," you can say, "as we agreed, you could have come home on time. But in making the decision not to be home on time, you also decided to stay home all next week. I'm sorry to see that you made this choice."

This example shows that honoring limits becomes an opportunity for the child to exercise control or influence. For maximum effect, it is important to avoid the adultisms that may come automatically to mind: "You know better than that. How can you be so irresponsible? If you are going to act like a child, then you will be treated like a child." The more effective approach is this:

"Honey, what was your understanding of what we agreed to on your curfew?"

The child might honestly be confused and respond, "I'm not sure."

This is an opportunity for clarification: "Your uncertainty shows me why we've had this problem. It's my recollection that you agreed to be home at twelve and that if anything happened that prevented this, you would call us to let us know what had taken place. Do you remember that?"

"I remember that now."

"What was your understanding of what we agreed would happen if you decided not to be home at twelve?"

"I'd have to stay home for the rest of the week."

"I just wanted to be sure we both had the same understanding about why you won't be going out for the rest of the week."

Compare this response to "OK, for you, you little sucker, that's it for this week. I'm going to fix your wagon forever!" In the latter, the child becomes a passive victim of an overwrought parent. In the former, the child's perception of having control remains in effect.

We may not realize how we invite the hassling from children that irritates us so much. We do this by setting limits we don't respect and threatening children with things that we don't deliver. We often say things we don't mean, such as "I can't afford it." What does "I can't afford it" mean to children who have never had to do without and have found that most of the things that they want come without a struggle?

When a child says she wants a new bicycle, and her father says he can't afford it, she wonders, "What on earth could Daddy be saying to me?" She reflects on her experience and remembers, "The last three times Daddy said that he couldn't afford it, I hassled him until I got what I wanted. So he must mean that I haven't hassled him enough for him to make this a priority."

Father says, "I can't afford it."

And she says, "Hassle, hassle."

He reassures her, "No, dear, I really can't afford it this time."

And she says, "Hassle, hassle, hassle."

Finally, he says, "Look, the only way I can consider it is on my credit card, and it is full."

She thinks, "Now we're making progress. He's considering ways to get it for me. I'm very close." So she continues to hassle.

Father's last weapon is to say, "If I get this for you, you'll have to give up your allowance for three years."

She thinks to herself, "Well, last time I gave it up for two years and still haven't gone without a nickel for one day in my life, so that's no big deal."

She proceeds with hassle, hassle, hassle, and finally Father gives in.

What is her perception of how you get what you want? Wish for it, hassle for it long enough, and you can even overcome "I can't afford it."

GUIDELINES

IN CONSIDERING THE CONDITIONS FOR fostering the growth of an inner locus of control in our children, we have actually established some new guidelines. If we want our children to perceive that they have power over their lives, we must—above all—tell them the truth. We must not say "I can't afford it" unless we really can't afford it. If we mean "You haven't hassled me enough to make it a priority," then we need to be honest. That way they can hassle us with dignity and respect and in the end understand why it was that hassling produced the outcome they desired.

Next on our guidelines is the assertion that whenever possible we set reasonable limits in advance, and then respect the limits we have set. We avoid making threats or promising things we can't or won't follow through on. With utter honesty on our part and clear limits established on their behavior, our children have better opportunities to understand how their world is organized. It is just this understanding of the world that encourages the perception of influence.

An important corollary to limit setting is the establishing of responsibilities and privileges around the home to further reinforce children's perception of the control they have. In later chapters we will consider the importance of self-discipline and a sense of responsibility in reinforcing our children's perceptions of how they control their lives. Suffice it to say that children's sense of their power to affect their lives rests on their comprehension of cause and effect. It is therefore essential that we allow them to experience the consequences of their actions.

The EIAG process is an excellent way to help children explore the consequences of their choices. Exploring consequences is much different from imposing consequences. Exploring teaches an internal locus of control, while imposing teaches an external locus of control.

Too often parents impose a punishment (which they try to disguise by calling it a consequence) instead of allowing children to experience the consequences of their choices and then explore it by figuring out what happened, what caused it to happen, how they feel about it, how they can use this information in the future, and what they can do to solve the problem now.

In keeping with our insistence on the value of dialogue, it is important that we lead our children to believe that discussing a problem with someone may result in a better solution. If we leave no room for dialogue and negotiation and our behavior tells them their actions have no bearing on what happens in the family, they will believe the false messages our world conveys: that self-discipline, good judgment, and a sense of responsibility have no relevance at all and that all of us are powerless victims of the environment.

A person does not have to be given power and need not experience a great deal of independence to develop the perception that he or she can make a difference. The key element is a guide committed to exploring with the child the what, why, and how of experience. It is important that this guide understand that the child will not automatically understand his or her power to have an effect but will need practice in exercising power.

> The hallmarks of effective parenting are *firmness, dignity,* and *respect* in exercising necessary authority and providing appropriate guidelines to young people.

A number of research studies have shown correlations between a young person's probability of delinquency, violence, and drug use—and even their drug of choice—based on the dominant style of parental control they experience. The kind of parenting principles involved in developing capable young people, according to our work and research, begins with minimizing directing, rescuing, pampering, permissiveness, strictness, and waffling with respect to limits and controls. Then the emphasis is increased on the hallmarks of effective parenting: *firmness, dignity,* and *respect* in exercising necessary authority and providing appropriate guidance to young people as they move toward autonomy.

Many parents and teachers are afraid to give up their controlling, authoritarian methods because they believe the only alternative is irresponsible permissiveness. Other parents and teachers are afraid to give up their permissiveness because they believe the only alternative is hostile tyranny. But the concepts we discuss in this book are based on the premise of firmness with dignity and respect—and this approach has proven effective where other behaviors across the spectrum are guaranteed to fail. The formula "Firmness plus dignity and respect" enables the parent to maintain control and responsibility but quickly brings children along to share in both. In the process, two goals are accomplished: Children develop the Significant Seven perceptions that yield capabilities, and parenting and teaching become easier over the long run. As one teacher said, "Learning to use these methods has relieved me of the despised roles of policeman, judge, jury, and executioner. Now I have time to teach."

FAMILY MEETINGS

FAMILY MEETINGS, DISCUSSED IN THE preceding chapter, offer fertile opportunities for fostering the growth of a sense of control in young people because they teach children that their input can make a difference. Successful family meetings require total family involvement, with everyone feeling needed and significant. Feelings of closeness, trust, and cooperation are pre-requisites for satisfying meetings. With these requirements met, such meetings enable family members to learn to work together in ways that are beneficial to everyone. That meetings are also an effective means of solving problems is an important fringe benefit.

An important part of the family meeting process is having an agenda displayed prominently where all family members can write the things they would like to discuss. You might stick up a piece of paper on the refrigerator where suggestions can be written during the week. Young people can develop perceptions of control simply by knowing they can suggest points to be discussed.

Only when decisions are made by consensus can family meetings be successful. Otherwise, children perceive them as a way for parents to manipulate and control. When conflicts arise that cannot be resolved, they should be tabled for a week and discussed again—and for as many times as it takes to reach a consensus. In Jane's family, the question of acquiring a dog was an active issue at family meetings for six months. The children wanted a dog, but the parents did not. The parents presented their concern: They would be left with all the work of feeding, caring for, and cleaning up after the dog. The children assured them that they would take full responsibility. The parents finally conceded when the children agreed to one condition: the dog would be given away if the children failed to meet their commitment to take full responsibility. The family bought a dog but gave it away a month later because the children failed to keep their promise. This was a very difficult lesson to learn, even though it was carried out with firmness, dignity, and respect. The family continued to discuss the dog question for another six months before the parents agreed to try again. This time, the children were diligent in taking care of the dog, because they knew what the consequences would be of failing to live up to their agreement. They knew their actions would affect their world.

The notion of returning again and again to the same subjects is an important one: The adults in the family must be prepared to do it. Jane's family discussed the issue of chores about every three weeks. After each discussion, the children enthusiastically adhered to the plan they come up with for doing their chores for about two or three weeks, and then they quit. When chores showed up on the agenda again, sometimes they devised another plan, and sometimes they decided to use the old plan with renewed commitment.

One question that arises frequently is whether family meetings make sense in single-parent families. The answer is an unqualified yes! The benefits are the same no matter how many people are in a family.

One of the primary benefits of family meetings is the closeness and connection that can be created when they are conducted with dignity and respect for all concerned. The whole family will benefit if parents make it clear that family time (and family meetings) is a priority on their calendars. Our children need to know that they are more important than other distractions and material things.

THE PERILS OF AFFLUENCE

IRONICALLY, AFFLUENCE HAS BECOME A serious problem in our society, especially in the realm of child rearing. When parents meet all the needs of their children, they rob them of the chance to develop an internal locus of control and thus become independent. Therefore, where parents are in the position to give their children "everything I didn't have," it is imperative that they find ways to involve their children creatively in the work it takes to go "first class." Wise parents provide economy-class accommodations and then charge tolls in time and effort when children ask for more.

When Steve's children ask for jeans, for example, he is willing to provide for good solid basics with no questions asked. However, many young people today expect more than basics—in this case, expensive designer jeans. To his daughter's plea for a pair, Steve replied, "Listen, honey, I got into the parenting deal to cover your body, not to decorate it, and I've discovered I can cover it for about $18."

The girl was horrified. "Dad, I can't wear $18 jeans. They're generic to the max. Don't be a terminal nerd."

He answered, "I don't understand that. What I understand is that there are wants and there are needs. What you want is style; what you need is modesty. When you ask me to consider style, you are asking for $25 more. I have the money—that is not the issue. The issue is that you are asking me to place de-signer jeans ahead of energy costs, school tuition, and retirement. The only way I can provide for those exigencies and still come up with style would be to make other adjustments in my life—for instance, parking the car and walking to work for several days to save gas money and to pass up lunch for a few days. It occurs to me that if you went without lunch for a few days, the jeans might fit better when you got them anyway.

"Still, I know you are working hard, and you keep assuring me that you are mature and able to take initiative. This time, how about meeting me halfway, perhaps by giving up a couple of movies or paying for gas for the car this week? If not, I'd just as soon go with modesty now and be done with it."

A few weeks later his daughter rushed up to Steve and said accusingly, "Dad, you have new ostrich skin boots."

He said, "Exactly. And I put in a fair bit of extra time and effort to earn them. I'm not opposed to enjoying nice things; I'm just opposed to being the only one in the family to put forth extra time and effort and to compromise priorities so you can enjoy them."

Weaning, not neglect, is the point here. If our children are to take control of their lives, they need to practice independence within the family. In a differ-ent way, weaning is a concept that should also be used in regard to television.

SUBSTITUTES FOR TELEVISION

TELEVISION WATCHING IS ONE ROUTINE that could be discussed during a family meeting. We have discussed how harmful the influence of television can be when children are overly exposed to the five themes of television —self-medication, drinking, casual sexuality, expedient acts of violence, and miraculous solutions to problems within a short time span—and the toll it takes on family closeness and connections.

Most families do not devise a plan for watching television. Instead, they just have the television on most of the time and watch whatever happens to be on. People will often switch stations over and over again looking for something decent to watch, but when they can't find anything good, they simply watch the best of the worst.

It would be much better to decide during family meetings how much television will be allowed. We suggest one to three hours per day, with flexibility for special programs. Since most children watch six to eight hours of television a day, this would be a real improvement. During a planning session, allow children to choose from a television guide which programs they really want to watch, and then keep the television off the rest of the time. If you have only one television set and different members of the family want to watch different programs, develop a plan for compromise. Perhaps each member can have first choice on different days.

> When we don't allow people to effect changes in their lives and hold them accountable for their actions and the results of their actions, we reinforce the perception "It's fate when I don't make it, luck when I do, but either way there was little that I had to do with it."

We also suggest that you sit and watch some programs with your children and discuss their perceptions of what they have seen after the program.

It is also important to involve the family in planning for other things to do during the time they have been used to watching television. It can be very scary to simply announce, "We are no longer going to watch so much television." This approach can cause a great deal of anxiety. When people have not been used to talking with each other, being together without the distraction of the television can be very awkward.

One mother gathered her children and the neighborhood children outside and taught them to play some of the group games she once played as a child such as Kick the Can and Hide and Seek.

Other families have planned to play Monopoly and other board games, play charades, take trips to the library, listen to motivational tapes and then discuss them, read classic books out loud, or do exercises together.

LIMITS AND CONSEQUENCES ENCOURAGE A BELIEF IN INTERNAL LOCUS OF CONTROL

WHEN WE DON'T ALLOW PEOPLE to effect changes in their lives and hold them accountable for their actions and the results of their actions, we reinforce the perception "It's fate when I don't make it, luck when I do, but either way there was little that I had to do with it."

By avoiding the barriers and using the builders described in chapter 4, we also encourage people to see their own influence over their lives.

Even the EIAG principles emphasized in the previous chapters are very effective when focused on individual actions, choices, and efforts:

"What caused you to do that?"
"What other options did you have?"
"How do you plan to deal with the situation now?"

These are excellent questions that reflect a belief in people's potency or influence over their life experiences. When young people sense our belief in them through our use of the EIAG process and the other activities explained in this chapter, they will feel the support that can be so important in helping them develop a perception of having influence over their lives.

7

Fostering Strong Intrapersonal Skills

T HE FOURTH PRINCIPLE of the Significant Seven helps children develop strong skills for handling their inner feelings, thoughts, and emotions in ways that increase their enjoyment of life and contribute to their success. There are three primary intrapersonal skills—that is, skills for managing our emotional lives:

1. Self-assessment
2. Self-control
3. Self-discipline

In a recent bestselling book called *Emotional Intelligence,* Daniel Goleman presents a comprehensive analysis of research in the areas of intra- and interpersonal skills and effectiveness. He uses the term *emotional intelligence,* or *EQ,* to describe the area under consideration. According to work in this area, our EQ has more to do with our personal success, relationships, and academic achievement than does our IQ!

If we think about it, this is sort of a "no-brainer." Most of us know someone with very high IQ who is undisciplined and unfocused and seldom accomplishes much beyond arrogance and/or delusional living. On the other hand, most of us also know someone who has average or below-average IQ yet is focused, self-disciplined, and effective with other people, who consistently accomplishes much more that would be expected. Much evidence also suggests that the earlier these resources are cultivated, the more profound and lasting the effects are on peoples' lives.

SELF-ASSESSMENT

SELF-ASSESSMENT IS THE ABILITY to recognize, interpret, and acknowledge personal feelings such as frustration, anger, joy, happiness, excitement, and love. This capability requires that one develops a vocabulary with which to express these feelings. All self-assessment statements begin with *I:* "I am excited," "I am upset," "I am frustrated," and "I am angry." Adults can help children learn this language by asking questions that invite self-assessment: "What do you think? What did that mean to you? How do you feel about that? How was that important to you?" In these questions, you'll recognize the EIAG principle.

Parents discourage self-assessment when they say, for example, "We don't get angry in this house! We don't yell! Go to your room right now, if you can't control yourself!" Telling young people what they can and can't feel teaches them to deny or hide their emotions. Further, parents who exhort their children with "Control yourself!" have often lost control of their own emotions.

> Once children become comfortable with the notion that their feelings are, as are the feelings of others, a legitimate, worthy part of their lives, they are ready to take the next step—to self-control.

Otherwise, instead of becoming caught up in their children's emotions, they would be able to observe with empathy what their children are experiencing and offer them gentle guidance in resolving their conflicts. Such empathetic observation and gentle guidance might be expressed as follows: "I don't blame you for being angry. I would be, too. I can't let you hit your sister, but I will talk with you about the problem in a little while when you've settled down and feel a little better." This example shows how we can allow children to experience their feelings as legitimate and give them feedback, while still setting limits on how their feelings may be expressed.

Also reflected in the example is the fact that the empathetic parent models self-assessment, self-control, and self-discipline by refusing to use unproductive time—when the emotions are out of control—to discuss and deal with the emotions. Angry people cannot learn about assessing and resolving their anger. The best time to discuss an angry moment is soon enough after the incident to recall the emotion but long enough afterward to permit objectivity.

It is useful to give children access to our own feelings as well as to focus on theirs. To do so, we can use such statements as "I'm feeling too angry to talk right now. I need to take a walk. I'll talk with you later when I've calmed down." Note that with such expressions we are not trying to displace the blame onto others, as we would be doing with "You made me angry" or "You made me upset." The point is to emphasize the situation and our own responsibility. Here's another good model expression: "I'm really angry about what has happened, so this is not a good time to talk about it. When I've thought about it some more, I'll come and find you." The goal is to allow our children to participate in our moments of high emotion without being made to feel responsible for them. However, when—as does happen—we act inappropriately as a result of our anger and humiliate or blame our children for our anger, it is effective to apologize: "I'm sorry I blamed you for my anger and said some disrespectful things to you. I have calmed down now and would like to discuss the situation rationally and work out some solutions with you." From our example, children can learn when it is appropriate to apologize.

Whenever we express a valid emotion, we should not apologize later by saying, "I'm sorry I was upset" or "I'm sorry I got angry." Our objective as parents should be to model self-control, self-assessment, and self-discipline through acknowledgment: "As you could tell, I was very upset over what happened. Now that I have settled down, I would like to go over it with you so that we both understand what happened."

Once children become comfortable with the notion that their feelings are, as are the feelings of others, a legitimate, worthy part of their lives, they are ready to take the next step—to self-control.

SELF-CONTROL

SELF-CONTROL IS THE ABILITY to select from among a number of possible behaviors an appropriate response to a feeling. It requires the recognition that feelings do not cause actions. Feelings are only feelings. Actions result from the choices the mind makes as to how to respond to the feelings.

A good way to practice exerting self-control is to evaluate a past behavior. For example, "I felt angry. I expressed my anger by hitting. What was the outcome? I was restricted, grounded, beaten up. Next time I'm angry, if I don't want that outcome to occur, what other behavior might I try? What else could I do with that anger besides precipitating a brawl?"

Children develop self-control when they learn to see the correlation between feelings and actions, actions and outcomes. The goal here is for them to understand "I feel . . . , I do . . . , I experience . . . . Next time I *feel* a certain emotion I might *do* something different so I can *experience* another outcome."

Start little children gently by asking, "What were you feeling? What did you do? What happened to you?" These questions, as you know, are designed to help them interpret an experience. With older children, we can begin to encourage them to project their understanding of feelings, behavior, and the link between the two.

We know children are ready to project into the future what they have learned when they stop asking, "Is it Saturday yet?" and are able to understand "It will be Saturday in three days." At that point, you can begin asking them, "When you feel . . . , what could you do, and what is likely to happen?"

When children are still saying, "Is this Saturday yet?" they are incapable of the kind of abstract thinking necessary for projecting. They can describe what just happened or what is happening, but they cannot predict their reactions to a hypothetical feeling. Nor can they explain their choices while they are experiencing an emotion. With older children and even with adults, stepping in and asking questions right in the middle of the anger will generally only promote more anger. With children, unless intervention is necessary to prevent clear and present harm, it is better to let an episode play itself out and then, when they are more in control, go back over the experience to help them understand.

Children aged six through eight are in the process of learning that their emotions need to be controlled. It is then that they can begin to understand that what they *choose* to do when they are angry, not what anger *makes* them do, is the issue.

As children become adept at generating and selecting from an array of behavior choices, they become able to impose the self between their feelings and actions. Thus, they gain self-control. Our goal is to help children understand that feelings are legitimate, that they have choices in handling their feelings, and that these choices have consequences. When they have this understanding, they are ready to go to the next level, which is self-discipline.

SELF-DISCIPLINE

SELF-DISCIPLINE IS THE ABILITY to consider an outcome in the abstract and then select a behavior that will achieve it. Another way of putting it is to say that self-discipline is the product of self-assessment and self-control in response to a given situation.

Self-assessment is summed up in the answers to these questions: "What do I most want to happen as a result of this experience? How would I like to feel when this is over?"

Self-control involves the understanding of the behaviors available. Self-discipline results when one is able to set aside behaviors that bring immediate gratification to achieve a chosen goal.

Children below age seven or eight years are not really capable of self-discipline. It is unreasonable to expect them to control their impulses and feelings. Through the EIAG process, we can teach them the consequences of giving in to feelings, but we shouldn't expect them to understand such a statement as this: "Even though I feel like hitting someone, I believe it would be best over the long term to sit down and talk it over." At about age eight, a response of this type becomes possible developmentally. The results after that age reflect the amount of training and reinforcement the child has received.

> Self-control involves the understanding of the behaviors available. Self-discipline results when one is able to set aside behaviors that bring immediate gratification to achieve a chosen goal.

PAMPERING AND SELF-DISCIPLINE

PAMPERING DIRECTLY INHIBITS THE DEVELOPMENT of self-discipline. Children learn only in an environment in which they have opportunities to deny themselves, bruise their knees, skin their shins, and break their hearts in little, temporary ways. In such an atmosphere, they can learn how to avoid breaking their necks, breaking their backs, and sustaining heartaches later in life.

Self-discipline can only be taught by parents who are mature enough and who love their children enough to avoid pampering them. Consider this

> We need to be tough enough in our love for our children to help them endure the temporary discomfort, upset, and even heartache it takes to begin learning the essential lessons of life.

example taken from Steve's dinner table. In the past, Steve and his wife made the mistake of calling to their son, "Mike, it's time to come in now and eat," and then keeping the boy's dinner warm. Often they called out to him several more times before going out to get him. They compounded the mistake by allowing Mike to enjoy a nice warm dinner while they lectured him about being inconsiderate.

If we are to raise capable children, we will call them once for dinner and then begin to eat. If they still hadn't arrived, we would clean up the mess and put away what is left. Later, when they would say, "Where's my dinner?" we would respond with love and support: "Honey, when it was time to eat, you felt like playing. Now you feel like eating, and it's time to play. So run on back outside and play. Tomorrow morning you'll have another chance to come to the table when you are called."

If we have the courage to respond in this way, within a couple of days, we'll begin to see self-discipline developing in our children. If not, all we'll get is an endurance contest to see who can hold out the longest.

We're looking for school teachers who will not say, "Mike, even though you didn't get your permission slip in for this field trip, go ahead and have a good time, honey, and bring it in on Monday." Allowing children to escape consequences in this way is something we can simply no longer afford. We need teachers who have the courage to say, "Mike, you didn't get your permission slip in for this field trip, so you can't go. I hope you remember to bring your slip next time so that you don't miss the next trip, too."

To put the point more broadly, we need to be tough enough in our love for our children to help them endure the temporary discomfort, upset, and even heartache it takes to begin learning the essential lessons of life. The following story exemplifies this fact:

> Steve came home one day recently, and his daughter passed him in the hall. "Hi, Daddy! Glad to see you. I'll be back in a little bit to talk." She was very happy and cheerful as she went on down the hallway. In a few minutes the next daughter came by and did very much the same thing. Then their mother came in. "Hi, honey, glad to see you. I've got to do a

couple of things. I'll be back in a couple of minutes." He heard her go down the hall and downstairs into the family room. He heard the daughters go in there, too. The next thing he heard was a racket of yelling, screaming, pounding feet up the stairs, and doors slamming.

Within a minute Steve's wife came into the bedroom, flopped down on the bed, and said, "That's it! I'm taking the American Express card and leaving. It's all up to you."

He gathered his courage and went downstairs to find out what was going on. The source of the problem wasn't hard to spot: a large pile of laundry stacked on the hide-a-bed in the middle of the family room. Apparently Mom went downstairs, found the pile of clothes, and became hostile and aggressive. She confronted the children, and they became manipulative and blaming. It wasn't an unusual situation. It had happened many times before. It was time to bring the problem to an end. So Steve and his wife decided to take the risk of letting the kids be responsible. They went out and bought four clothes hampers in different colors. Then they held a "workshop" on running the washer and dryer and folding clothes. Mom and Dad were getting out of the laundry business.

Of course, it turned out to be not quite so simple. Once they gave their lesson on running the washer and assigned each child a hamper, they had to have dialogue with each child: "Honey, now that we know you can run the washer and dryer and have a basket for your clothes, is there anything you can think of that would result in your leaving clothing on the hide-a-bed?"

Each of the children assured their parents that there was no reason for leaving clothing on the hide-a-bed anymore.

"Fine!" said the parents. "We will assume that any clothing left on the hide-a-bed now is surplus clothing that you are finished with. We'll gather it up and take it to Goodwill."

And they did! That's the important thing: they did! During the next week they gave away several sets of intimate apparel that had been casually left on the hide-a-bed. They gave away half of a new pair of socks. They gave away a highly cherished Spiderman shirt. By the end of the week the consensus of the children was "Mom and Dad are serious. If you want to keep your stuff, don't leave anything in the family room."

The learning continued over the next few weeks. About two weeks later, Steve's middle daughter said to him, "Daddy, Keri says I smell funny."

Steve said, "Come over here a minute and let me check this out." Sniff! "She's right! What could be causing that?"

"I don't know."

"Well, how are things going with your hamper and the washer and dryer?"

"I haven't used them yet."

"Well, that could be part of the problem."

"How do I know when clothes need to be washed? Mom always took care of that before."

So that was the problem: Mom always took care of that before. Steve said, "Maybe you're too close to the problem to understand it. Why don't you take your clothes off here, go over and stand in the doorway, get some fresh air, and come back and check them out."

When she came back she said, "They do smell funny."

"Well, what are your choices?"

"Instead of going out to play, I'd better stay in and get my clothes washed or nobody will want to play with me, anyway." She had learned a lesson.

A few days later, Steve's oldest daughter went through her learning process. She was in the eighth grade and the top class in junior high school. The school year was coming to an end. Next year, she would be at the bottom of the heap as a freshman in high school. So her plan was to capitalize on her power at the last dance of the school year and go out in a blaze of glory.

The first step was to manipulate Dad into buying her a dress he could scarcely afford. She took the dress to church, showcasing it, and raised two or three eyebrows. She now knew it had the desired effect. She was ready. Her plan was to have her hair done on Friday. She had saved up her skating money for a couple of weeks so she could afford it. She figured that between the new dress and the fine new hair-do, she would really knock 'em dead.

Friday came, she went off to have her hair done, came home to get ready for the dance, and couldn't find her new dress anywhere. She searched around for it and finally found this beautiful dress right where she had left it after church that Sunday—in the bottom of the clothes hamper, all mildewed, stained, and blotched. And she couldn't wear it. So off she went to the biggest dance of her life in a hodgepodge that didn't excite anybody.

The next day she went to Steve, "Daddy, how long can you leave a dress in the hamper before it gets mildewed?"

Steve said, "Well, this time of the year, with wet swimming suits and towels and stuff, that can happen overnight."

"Gee, I didn't know that. Mom always looked after the clothes before. How could I know, Dad? I ruined the dress. I'd better go through the hamper every night and get my stuff out of there, or it's all going to get ruined with these little kids around."

And she learned. The learning took place because she had a chance to affect important things in her life through the decisions she made (or did not make) concerning her own clothes. Each of the children learned the lesson, and none forgot it.

PRIVILEGES AND RESPONSIBILITIES

WHILE SELF-DISCIPLINE IS THE ABILITY to control emotions, *responsibility* is the ability to recognize and understand limits and consequences, earned privileges and responsibilities—in short, cause and effect as it operates in the world. Self-discipline that is not coupled with a sense of responsibility can have catastrophic results, for the latter limits the former. For example, some people are so self-disciplined that they are irresponsible with their health and their relationships with people around them. Anorexia, for example, may (to a degree) reflect self-discipline taken to pathological extremes. The failure to share feelings can be a result of self-discipline unqualified by a sense of responsibility.

Responsibility, then, is a crucial element in the learning and maturing processes. Adults can help young people develop effective self-discipline and responsibility—that is, self-discipline tempered by an understanding of cause and effect—by ensuring that the children's privileges are directly related to their willingness to accept responsibility.

Adults can help young people develop effective self-discipline and responsibility—that is, self-discipline tempered by an understanding of cause and effect—by ensuring that the children's privileges are directly related to their willingness to accept responsibility.

As children grow, they become developmentally ready to accept greater responsibility. It is up to parents and teachers to see that their privileges match their particular developmental level.

For example, each of Jane's children at three years old was given very limited privileges regarding bedtime; the child could choose which pair of pajamas he or she wanted to wear. When they reached about nine years of age, the children were allowed to choose their own bedtimes. They could go to bed anytime they wanted as long as they accepted the responsibility of getting up in the morning by themselves—cheerfully—and getting themselves dressed, making their own lunches, eating their breakfasts, and getting to school on time without any help from their parents.

When these privileges and responsibilities came up at family meetings, the children agreed to them. The family discussed not only the consequences of the children not carrying out their responsibilities—losing the privilege of choosing bedtimes—but also strategies for successfully carrying them out. The children deliberated on how much time they would need to get ready in the morning and learned to set their own clock radios. Whenever a child reached the magic age, nine, the plan was tested again.

Each time it was very difficult for Jane to keep her mouth shut and let them succeed or fail without interference. She found it helpful to take long showers or long walks in the morning to avoid the temptation to remind or threaten.

Each child in turn was at first so excited about having the privilege of staying up late that he or she invariably stayed up until midnight. But it never took the children long to discover how difficult it was to get up cheerfully and to fulfill their responsibilities when they had not had enough sleep. Each had to learn the hard way by having the privilege rescinded for a while when he or she was just too tired to get up. In all such instances, Jane simply said, "I respect your decision to give up the privilege of choosing your own bedtime for a while. Let me know when you want to try it again." Sure enough, self-discipline merged with the newborn sense of responsibility, and, after some fits and starts, the system worked like clockwork.

THE SUPERPARENT

ANOTHER WAY TO HELP CHILDREN develop a sense of responsibility is to teach them the difference between needs and wants by meeting their needs and letting them fulfill their own wants. But too often superparents deny children the chance to participate.

A whole generation of parents learned too well the lessons of patience, self-discipline, self-sacrifice, delayed gratification, responsibility, and hard work. These parents did not realize the benefits of their own hard work. Instead, they thought it only right that they do literally everything for their children. In the process, they deprived them of the ingredients of self-reliance.

Today, one out of every five parents is secretly going through school again. How? By doing their children's homework. This could have something to do with the fact that achievement scores are going down nationwide. Children whose parents do their homework aren't learning anything except how to manipulate their parents. In previous generations, parents had no time to stay up late typing a paper while their children stood by, tearfully apologizing for forgetting it was due in the morning.

A single mother recently complained to us at a workshop, "I work two jobs and try to make it home to cook for my nineteen-year-old son, who won't shop or do the dishes. What should I do?"

Steve said, "Take this quarter, make a phone call, and tell your son you won't make it home tonight to cook his dinner."

She was horrified. "But what will happen?"

"I don't know, but I have seen teenagers become incredibly self-reliant when faced with starvation. Some have eaten plain bread. Some have opened cans of Spaghetti-Os and eaten them cold."

When we allow children to meet their needs solely by manipulating us, we also set them up for chemical dependency. Any other solution to dealing with life situations requires self-discipline, delayed gratification, sacrifice, and hard work. Earlier generations experienced affirmation and self-confidence as they learned how to contribute to family and society and to obtain what they wanted for themselves. The scarcity of such experiences for our youth today has created a crisis in self-confidence and self-esteem, since one of the surest ways to destroy these traits is to do so much for a person that he or she has no chance to have an effect.

Ungrateful children and suffering parents have become the order of the day, and both these symptoms are traceable to our fascination with providing material comforts. It is time to use our affluence wisely. We need to provide basic accommodations for our children and then structure their environment so they put in the time and effort necessary to stretch, but not break, themselves.

BARRIERS

THREE PRIMARY BARRIERS DISCOURAGE CHILDREN from developing the intrapersonal skills of self-assessment, self-control, and self-discipline. Each barrier is treated below in detail.

Barrier 1: Projecting Feelings onto Others

This is the language we use when we project our feelings onto others: "You make me angry." "You frustrate me." "You get me upset." This behavior is the opposite of self-assessment. It indicates that we fail to take responsibility for our own feelings and place the blame for those feelings elsewhere. The burden of other people's feelings is a heavy one to bear; yet we often load children down with that burden. Children onto whom we have projected our feelings assume they have tacit permission to project their feelings onto others. As long as others produce their feelings, there is no foundation for self-assessment or self-control, and they can therefore justify reacting to their environment rather than acting on it.

Psychotherapist Wayne Dyer tells the story of a client who claimed that her husband gave her an inferiority complex. Dr. Dyer asked, "Oh, how does he do that?"

The client said, "He tells me I am stupid."

Dr. Dyer said, "Well, knowing him, that does not surprise me. That sounds like the kind of thing he would say, but how does that make you stupid?"

She replied, "When he tells me I'm stupid, I feel stupid."

Dr. Dyer said, "Does that mean that if he comes home tonight and tells you you are a car, you will feel like a car?"

> Our feelings are our own, based on our individual perceptions, and they change as our perceptions change. In knowing this fact we find great freedom—and freedom plus responsibility equals independence.

The client laughed, "Of course not. I am not a car."

Dr. Dyer persisted, "Wait a minute. Suppose he brings a nozzle and wants to put gasoline in your ear. Then will you feel like a car?"

"Of course not," she said with confidence.

Dr. Dyer asked, "Then why do you feel you are stupid just because he says you are?"

This lady would refuse to feel like a car no matter what anyone else said, yet she was quick to believe she was stupid at the slightest suggestion from her husband. She allowed her husband to determine how she felt about herself and therefore functioned as a passive reactor, not an active decider and changer. Our feelings are our own, based on our individual perceptions, and they change as our perceptions change. In knowing this fact we find great freedom—and freedom plus responsibility equals independence.

Barrier 2: Using "Why?" as an Inquisition

The second primary barrier to the development of the intrapersonal skills is the expectation that our feelings are based on a rationale: "Why did you do that? Why do you feel that way? Why are you angry? Why are you frustrated? Why are you upset?" We constantly demand these things of others. The more reasonable demand is for an explanation of a given behavior: "What caused you to behave that way when you were angry? What were you trying to accomplish when you did that?" The answer might be complicated, it is true, but it could make sense. But any attempt to explain why we feel as we do would end in a muddle.

What we can do is describe our feelings and examine their link with actions. When we encourage children to do this, we foster the development of the intrapersonal skills. With these they can begin to answer the question, "Next time you are upset like that, what else might you do?"

Barrier 3: Doing Too Much for Children

The third barrier is characteristic of superparents. They continually rush to rescue their children from their inadequacies by compensating for them or by stepping in and deferring the consequences of their children's chosen behavior. And, as we have shown, this robs the children of their opportunity to learn that their behavior has consequences.

Consider this very typical example of rescuing. When a child says, "I'm bored," most middle-class parents take that statement as an indictment of their own parenting abilities. There is a prevailing belief that no American child should ever know boredom or an unprogrammed or unoccupied moment. If we respond to "I'm bored" with "Why don't you do this? What about this?" we are taking responsibility for rescuing the child from boredom. In so doing, we are teaching the child simply to declare boredom and then sit back and wait to be entertained. Rescuing parents respond this way: "Maybe we can design a youth center. How about going to a movie? What if I buy you a new car? Could I interest you in a ski trip to Colorado?" Teaching children to hold out for the highest ante, these parents run around in terror trying to organize their children's lives. Children do not learn to be assertive and creative when parents handle all their problems for them. Rescuing works directly against creativity, self-actualization, and self-reliance.

> Children who can assess their feelings and select their reactions with an eye to achieving a chosen goal are on the path toward effectiveness in a complex world rich with opportunity.

The responsible parent trying to develop a successful child would respond to "I'm bored" by saying, "I believe I understand a little bit about what you are feeling, Son. I hope it works out," and then would walk away briskly to avoid further attempts at manipulation. We have never known children who, if allowed to be bored for an hour, didn't become so bored with boredom that they began to exercise their native intelligence and come up with a creative menu of things to occupy their time.

Boredom or other crises in feeling are rich opportunities for development. Once the intense feeling has passed, parents can explore the incident gently and thoughtfully, using the EIAG process. "What were you feeling? What did you do in response to that feeling? Then what happened? If you wanted the same thing to happen next time you have that feeling, what would you do? How would you handle your anger differently if you wanted something else to happen?"

Once children begin to ask themselves, "What do other people do with their feelings?" they can generate a selection of alternatives. With respect to anger, for instance, they could say, "When I feel angry I could walk away, step outside, stay away from home until I've cooled off, or wait a little while before I confront anyone." With several alternate behaviors to consider, their chances for acting in an appropriate and productive way will increase immeasurably. Children who can assess their feelings and select their reactions with an eye to achieving a chosen goal are on the path toward effectiveness in a complex world rich with opportunity.

8

Fostering Strong Interpersonal Skills

ONE OF THE greatest struggles people have involves learning how to interact with others. For young people, a deficit in these skills leaves them unable to function well. The result in children who are unable to make themselves understood and appreciated is a sense of impotence, hostility, and even rage. The fifth principle in the Significant Seven involves helping children develop the interpersonal skills they need to interact effectively.

As our world experiences radical changes due to an explosion of knowledge and technology, we find that interpersonal skills are now identified by employers as the most critical skill area for the modern workplace. They are essential to customer service, management, training, and conflict resolution. These skills are essential to building and maintaining healthy relationships. Evidence also shows that they may be foundational to reading readiness and effective learning. Tragically, evidence indicates, too, that (for too many of us and our children) these skills are developing more slowly and less adequately than in previous eras. Much of the delay seems to be influenced by lifestyle changes such as the decline in dialogue and interaction between family and extended family members and the increasing dominance of technology during critical developmental periods for children.

INTERPERSONAL SKILLS NECESSARY FOR EFFECTIVE SOCIAL INTERACTION

Listed here are the interpersonal skills necessary for effective social interaction, followed by brief descriptions of what each entails:

Ability	Definition
Listening	Understanding what others are saying from their point of view
Communicating	Exchanging ideas with others
Cooperating	Working with others toward a common goal
Negotiating	Resolving conflicts with others in a process of give and take
Sharing	Including others in one's experiences and activities
Empathizing	Conveying an understanding of others' feelings or needs

LISTENING SKILLS

THE FOUNDATION OF INTERPERSONAL SKILLS is the ability to initiate and maintain a meaningful exchange of perceptions. For such an exchange to take place, we must be able to listen actively and effectively. At the present time, listening is the most underdeveloped capability in our culture. Effective listening is the ability to form an image in our minds of what people are saying to us—to actively analyze and confirm it so that in our minds we are able to change places with the other person and spontaneously appreciate his or her point of view.

The ability to listen effectively requires a special kind of training that is not being administered to young children today. This is in spite of the fact that listening skills, along with those for engaging in dialogue, are the foundation skills for, among other things, reading. After years of studying remedial programs, we found that it is difficult to teach reading comprehension to a poor listener. Reading seems to be less a primary skill than a product of other skills. Essentially, it is a form of dialogue.

Important among the listener's tools are the abilities (1) to paraphrase and (2) to use "I" statements. Together these skills enable us to determine whether we have understood a message accurately. Here are some examples of paraphrasing at work: "I am not sure I understood what you were saying; was it [paraphrase]?" or "What I heard you say was [paraphrase]."

Important among the listener's tools are the abilities (1) to paraphrase and (2) to use "I" statements. Together these skills enable us to determine whether we have understood a message accurately.

The biggest mistake people make when they attempt paraphrasing is to parrot the words that have been said rather than listening for and then paraphrasing the feeling or meaning behind the words.

For example, a child may complain, "You are never home." An effective paraphrase might be "You wish I were more available for you?" or "You would like for us to have more time with each other?" A paraphrase should always be a question to check whether you have understood what was meant.

Though "I" statements used too liberally can make one's conversation seem superficial and insincere, used sparingly they can ensure effective dialogue. A good example of an "I" statement is "Let me check with you to make sure I've caught your meaning."

Another important listening skill involves weighing the message in light of our previous experience with the speaker. To avoid stereotyping, it is important to acknowledge similarities with old messages while still listening for new meanings. Too often, we ignore the message of familiar people, because we tend to "hear" what we expect them to say.

To test a message, we need to look first at content (the *what* of the message) and then at the speaker's motivation (the *why* of the message). When we listen for both, we go a long way toward ensuring that we will understand them accurately. Taking care to listen in this way not only facilitates our own active communication but also models effective communication techniques to our children. This approach, combined with a scrupulous avoidance of adultisms and assumptions regarding the other's meaning, shows children how to interrelate effectively.

In talking with your children, slow them down with such comments as "Let me be sure I understand what you've been saying to me." In doing so, you will be showing them both how to attend to content and how to respect the speaker enough to check the accuracy of their understanding. A beneficial side effect, of course, is that you will be conveying your own respect for the content and motivation of your child's messages.

NEGOTIATING

PARAPHRASING FOR CHECKING PURPOSES IS also a negotiating skill. People cannot reach an understanding without having clarity regarding each other's point of view. Children need to be taught to respond to calls for clarification—"Let me be sure you understand what I was asking you to do"—and to make their own clarifying calls.

Negotiation is based on mutual respect. We show our respect for our children when we permit flexibility in a situation at home. Regarding curfew, for instance, we might say, "I know your activities vary, and sometimes you have to travel farther than others, so setting a single curfew time is unreasonable. So let's work out a flexible agreement, and then we'll both abide by it."

Our willingness to be flexible also teaches young people that we respect their feelings and encourages them to respect those of others. In addition, by modeling good communication, we encourage our children to explore and appreciate others' feelings.

REDUCING INTERACTIONS TO MULTIPLE-CHOICE EXAMS

IRONICALLY, THE MULTIPLE-CHOICE EXAM, a teaching method widely used in schools today, may actually increase passivity and minimize the affirmation, validation, and encouragement our children should receive. Parents can compound the problem of passivity in children by reducing their own communications to multiple-choice or true/false quizzes by means of adultisms: "Did you? Can you? Do you? Will you? Won't you? Are you? Aren't you?" or, as they get a little older, "Why can't you ever? How come you never? Surely you realize! How many times do I have to tell you? When will you ever grow up?" Such questions and statements all create an atmosphere of threat and breed a sense of inadequacy in children. Knowing that their response will be discounted, criticized, or dismissed is a good reason not to offer one. To have true dialogue, it is not simply enough to exchange information; the exchange must take place in a climate of support and interest.

Studies of adults who interact with children consistently show that most of them assume that children lack the verbal skills and insight necessary to answer thoughtful questions for themselves. When adults make that assumption, they often answer the questions for children and thereby invalidate the children as thinking, feeling individuals. And the kinds of questions they ask children tend to reinforce this destructive attitude. "Did you have a good day? Was that fun for you? Do you like this doll? Are you enjoying yourself?" All these are close-ended questions that can be answered with a yes, no, or "I don't know." True stimulation comes from open-ended questions: "What feelings do you have about this?" "What kinds of things were fun for you?" "What was good about your day?" "Tell me about your favorite doll." "What did you learn today?"

In a recent study involving so-called deprived, inner-city preschool children, the practice of asking children close-ended questions was changed, with impressive results. The researchers taught adults to ask, "What things were fun for you today?" and "What did you learn?" instead of "Did you have fun today?" and "Did you learn anything today?" In addition, they taught the adults the importance of being patient after asking open-ended questions to give the children time to return thoughtful responses. These researchers found that when they were able to increase the total stimulation in this way by an average of seven minutes a day, or a total of one hour per week, testable IQ rose by an average of eight points for boys and girls between the ages of four and five. When these same children started school, they were more confident, self-assured, and effective in responding to teachers than children who had not been so stimulated. Furthermore, they showed more closeness, trust, and involvement with those adults who were significant in their lives. Clearly, dialogue is a very powerful strategy for affirming, validating, and encouraging even very young children.

Still, our efforts and expectations must match children's developmental levels. Children's perceptual abilities change as they grow and develop. Expectations that exceed the child's developmental abilities are perceived by the children as serious threats. On the other hand, children who are not expected to use the abilities they have can become extremely discouraged. If we are always saying, "Don't do that," "You are too little," or "Never try to get something without checking with me," we are conveying the subliminal message "I have absolutely no confidence in your ability to do things for yourself." This lack of confidence will create dependent people who, when we later criticize them for not taking more responsibility, will be paralyzed by a double bind. Children initially learn a great deal about themselves from our interactions with them. At about age five, they begin to act on what they believe about themselves. And just at this critical point, rather than allowing them to continue to develop clarity in a familiar environment, we send them off to the unfamiliar surroundings of school. Over the next two or three years, with no basic experience to draw from, they again become quite vulnerable in their interactions with adults. If they find themselves among closed, judgmental people who discount what they think or believe, children will learn to be passive and tentative in offering anything. If they are fortunate enough to be among affirming people who know how to encourage them to explore ideas, they will become increasingly confident, assertive, and skilled in interacting with others.

PUBERTY AND THE DEVELOPMENTAL PROCESS

AS THEY APPROACH THE AGE of ten, children begin to develop a sense of personal identity. This identity is a result of the accumulation of perceptions about their place in the world. Children in this age range are amusingly clear in their perceptions of the world. They begin to draw conclusions from their experiences and perceptions and to develop absolutes and other consistent thought patterns. Suddenly, they feel certain that they know how life works. "We are Presbyterians. They are Catholics. We don't eat pizza. We don't have those kinds of friends. We don't watch those kinds of shows." There is little equivocation in the mind of a ten-year-old.

But no sooner do they get a grip on life and begin to act with some sense of consistency than what happens? Massive doses of testosterone and progesterone come roaring through their bodies to wipe out all their certainty. Their bodies tingling with hormonal revolt, they must start to reassess all over again who they are and how life works. They have new bodies, new moods, new feelings, and new impulses. By the age of twelve, most have a six-year gap between their minds and their bodies. This gap exists throughout adolescence.

> Very frequently, parents fail to understand that children who lie and misrepresent themselves are usually doing so because they want their parents to think well of them.

In one family we know, the first-born daughter has an eighteen-year-old physical plant with an eleven-year-old board of trustees directing her around town. Right behind her comes another daughter who, at age fifteen, is intellectually precocious; she has a twenty-year-old mind trapped in an eleven-year-old, prepubescent body without a curve or hair anywhere in sight. One girl looks down at her body and says, "Will this ever stop?" The other one, looking in the same direction, says, "Will anything ever start?" Such concerns can be very distracting, to say the least.

By the age of thirteen, life has become immediate and turbulent. For thirteen-year-olds, the longest-term goal often has a life span of three hours. A life's dream frequently lasts a week. Children of this age can be in hopeless ecstasy one minute and in terminal depression the next. And the source of their despair can be a single skin blemish. "I'll die if this big dipper is still here on Saturday!" you might hear them moan.

Parents can be very discouraging to adolescents who are in such throes. In the midst of these new bumps and hairs, parents step in anxiously and intensify the problem with "Why can't you ever? How come you never? Surely you realize! How many times do I have to tell you? When will you ever grow up? You knew better than that! You are too big to behave this way." From such adultisms young people infer their parents to say, "I have been accumulating data on your inadequacies for years, so this doesn't surprise me at all. In addition to all the new changes that have made you feel awkward, there is a large shopping list of ideas and expectations you don't comprehend, so you must be in worse shape than you think." Is it any wonder that children in turmoil distrust their disapproving parents? Instead, these children will likely think, "You are the last person I can confide in because I want you to think well of me, and yet I'm rapidly using up all my approved credit with you."

> By neglecting to understand their children's perceptions, parents drive the children deeper and deeper into irrational behavior.

Adultisms are perceived as threats, and perceived threat produces a sense of powerlessness and despair. In the face of them, children who want us to love and accept them begin to lie and misrepresent themselves. Very frequently, parents fail to understand that children who lie and misrepresent themselves are usually doing so because they want their parents to think well of them.

WHY LYING CAN MAKE SENSE

WE'VE SEEN FROM THE PRIOR discussion that lying becomes prevalent with the onset of puberty. Teenagers who are insecure about their identity feel that they aren't living up to adults' expectations. Also, they are sorting through changing bodies, bewildering emotions, and new feelings. When adults respond with adultisms, they drive children away from them and into the arms of their peers.

Children around the age of six to eight lie when they are anxious to exert their independence and still want the approving love and security of their parents. Frequently, they think they can behave as they choose, as long as they cover up their tracks by lying.

Parents often misinterpret the reasons behind the lying. As a result, they punish the children harder and become more judgmental and hostile. Too often, they forget that children base their behavior on what *they* perceive as reality, not on their parents' perceptions of reality. By neglecting to understand their children's perceptions, parents drive the children deeper and deeper into irrational behavior. Thus, it is the parents who can create a threatening environment. Under such conditions, effective communication, cooperation, negotiation, and problem solving cannot effectively take place.

DEPARTMENT STORE SEMINAR

IN A DEPARTMENT STORE RECENTLY, Steve saw a miniseminar in interpersonal skills. A mother rushed up to her daughter and demanded, "How many times do I have to tell you not to touch the toys?"

The child answered, "Eleven!"

The mother lost it right there. "What do you mean, eleven?" she yelled.

"I don't know," said the child.

As we have seen, "I don't know" is often the only safe answer. This child had already learned that the last thing her parent wanted was a thoughtful response. What her mother *really* wanted was to make her feel dumb, inadequate, and childish.

At the checkout stand, Steve saw an even more advanced seminar in relationships. There was a thirteen-year-old boy who had obviously started puberty but who hadn't gone anywhere with it yet. Just as Steve joined the line, the boy's father said, "Why are you angry?"

Steve wanted to drop to his knees and give this father an honest answer on behalf of the boy: "Because a passing frontal system has upset the pressure gradient in ways that are producing subtle changes in your son's limbic system. That, together with the overabundance of highly processed starch, sugar, fats, and carbohydrates that he was saturated with at lunch and the frustration of trying to contain all those ambient calories without moving, wiggling, or fidgeting through three hours of classes, created a lot of pent-up energy and frustration that he carried onto the school bus. There he was told to 'Sit down. Shut up. Close the window. Pipe down. I'm going to tell your parents. You are going to get a suspension for this.' Your son then stepped off the bus with all that going on and added a dose of caffeine and sugar from a Pepsi plus theo-bromine from a brownie, which went roaring up through the inherited insta-bility of his hypothalamus from three generations of alcoholics in his pedigree—not to mention the normal instability due to puberty. All of this turbulence then bounced off a massive dose of testosterone flowing through him, which greatly magnified the frustration of trying to meet and anticipate adult expectations all day. In short, it was more than he could handle."

The boy himself said simply, "Because!"

The father said, "What do you mean, 'because'?"

And the boy gave back, "I don't know"—the only safe answer.

NO PANTS

WHEN STEVE APPROACHED HIS HOME, he heard yet another seminar going on at his neighbor's house, whose open window was a good source of material for Steve's workshops. This time what came through the window was this: "Where are my brown pants? You knew I would need them for my next trip. Every week, it's the same thing. Nothing is ready. I can't earn a living naked."

Compare these exasperated explosives with "Honey, what was your under-standing of what I planned to take with me on this trip?"

"To tell you the truth, we never discussed it."

"Ah, that could explain why my brown pants aren't here."

"As far as I know, you never took them to the cleaners, did you?"

"I thought you were going to do that."

"Well, dear, you've been so fussy about your pants for the last few weeks, I just knew you would want to handle them yourself. I'll tell you what. If it's real important to you, I'll drop them off this week, and they'll be here for your next trip."

In either case, the neighbor has no brown pants! But if he continues with the first method, he soon will have no wife, no children, and no closet to put his pants in. Instead, he will have alimony, child support, an efficiency apartment, and a therapist.

Back in the department store, couldn't the mother have said to the four-year-old, "Honey, what was your understanding of what I asked you to do with the toys?" If she kept on in this mode, she would soon have had a child who dealt with her happily and openly rather than one who ran around the store testing unmarked boundaries.

What about the father at the checkout stand? Couldn't he have said, "I can see you are very upset, Son," instead of requiring the boy to be articulate about feelings he had never had before? "When you settle down, I would like to go over the day with you to make sure I understand what caused the problem." This response is respectful and shows a recognition of the young person's struggle. It conveys empathy without requiring an articulate response at a time when the boy is struggling for control and self-understanding. This response on the parent's part is not demeaning. It allows the child to preserve his dignity yet communicates interest and concern. It also models communication, empathy, good listening, and other interpersonal skills and encourages their development in the child.

BARRIERS TO THE DEVELOPMENT OF INTERPERSONAL SKILLS

HERE ARE THE BARRIERS THAT inhibit the development of interpersonal skills.

Barrier 1: Lack of Respect for Unique Perceptions

One great inhibitor is the lack of respect parents show for their children's unique perceptions. When we travel to another country, we do not get along very well if we spend our time criticizing the way the indigenous people do things. On the other hand, we broaden our knowledge and experience when we make every effort to understand, respect, and enjoy the differences we find.

In a way, each individual is a different culture. When we remember this and approach each individual with interest, respect, and a desire to learn about his or her unique way of viewing the world, we eliminate most of the conflict and frustration experienced in relationships.

Barrier 2: The Big Five

The five barriers discussed in chapter 4 are also counterproductive to the development of interpersonal skills. By removing those five barriers and developing a language that promotes dialogue, we not only make young people feel more capable but also encourage them to respond to us when we want to talk with them. Ultimately, in this way we trigger the development of strong interpersonal skills.

> The more time children spend in front of the television, the less skilled they become in dialogue.

Barrier 3: Television

Another barrier to the emergence of these skills is television. The more time children spend in front of the television, the less skilled they become in dialogue. In early childhood this lack of practice in dialogue is especially pernicious.

Most authorities recommend no more than six hours a week of exposure to television in a child's first six years of life. Any additional television time reduces the amount of time children spend actively formulating images, exchanging ideas, asserting themselves in the environment, and interacting with significant others—the primary developmental activities for this age group.

Recently the American Academy of Pediatrics, with over seventy members, took the unprecedented position of urging no television during the first two to three years and minimal exposure over the first twelve years. Although this is a very tall order and almost impossible to implement, it does underscore these doctors' concern about child development. They indicated that their position is based less on what is on TV (which has already been the focus of much debate and discussion) than it is on what is not happening, developmentally,

KEYS TO SUCCESS FOR DEVELOPING INTERPERSONAL SKILLS IN CHILDREN

Here's a summary of the keys to success in encouraging the growth of interpersonal skills in children:

1. Practice respectful dialogue.
2. In dealing with children, become skillful in listening, empathizing, and negotiating.
3. Structure as many situations as possible to require practice in these skills. Be patient and acknowledge successful as well as unsuccessful efforts on your part (we all make mistakes).

during the time devoted to it and other media. As an alternative, they recommended dialogue, storytelling, imaginative play, and interaction with people of different ages.

Barrier 4: Lack of Dialogue in Families

As stated often in this book, dialogue was once the primary activity in family life. Even if children weren't talking a great deal, they would listen to thoughts and ideas expressed by the real people (as opposed to television characters) they were identifying with and emulating. Today children are reduced to emulating fantasy figures and TV cops—and their parents wonder where they get all their bizarre ideas.

With enough experience and examples, young people will come to use their interpersonal skills spontaneously. They will resolve differences, work with others, understand others, and deal effectively with their own ideas, feelings, and needs.

9

Fostering Strong Systemic Skills

THE SIXTH OF the Significant Seven concepts helps children develop the systemic skills, which consist of having an understanding of cause and effect, responsibility, adaptability, and flexibility.

Systems are made of factors that are directly related to each other. Examples of systems are cause and effect, limits and consequences, privileges and responsibilities, principles of organization, and principles of physics. Notice that the components of these systems exist only in relation to each other. Without the other factor or factors with which they interrelate, they have no meaning or effect.

CAUSE AND EFFECT

CHILDREN NEED TO UNDERSTAND THE system of cause and effect to accept the inevitable conditions of—that is, the limits of—reality. When children have strong systemic skills and can thus understand and predict the way reality works, they can use their native creativity to work within its limits. Such an understanding is a component of leadership, high productivity, and the combined qualities we call genius. *Genius* is the ability to perceive unacknowledged or unknown relationships within the universe and to give them cohesion.

In the everyday realm, a clear understanding of cause and effect is necessary for the setting and achieving of goals. To set a goal, a child must be able to predict what outcomes are possible, what relationships are involved, and what steps must be taken with respect to those relationships for the goal to be achieved.

RESPONSIBILITY

AT THE CORE OF THE systemic skills is a sense of *responsibility*—the ability to recognize and act appropriately with regard to the interrelated components of the environment. A responsible person is one who perceives the interrelationships among the elements and principles constituting their world and is able to work with them effectively.

For example, if a child throws a rock and breaks a window, grounding or a spanking won't teach responsibility. EIAG and a logical consequence will.

> A responsible person is one who perceives the interrelationships among the elements and principles constituting their world and is able to work with them effectively.

"What were you thinking of when you threw the rock?"

"I didn't know it would break the window."

"So you were a scientist without even meaning to be. What did you learn from your experiment?"

"I broke the window."

"What will you do next time?"

"Won't throw rocks."

"What do you now need to do about the window?"

"I can't fix it."

"How will it get fixed?"

"The glass man."

"Who will pay?"

"I don't know."

"Who broke it?"

"I did."

"Who do you think should pay?"

"Maybe I should, but I don't have enough money."

"Do you have any ideas on what you could do about that?"

"Well, I suppose you could deduct the cost of the window from my allowance."

"Good idea! When we find out how much it costs, I will help you figure out how long it will take for you to deduct enough money from your allowance to pay for it."

Some parents define a responsible child as a "perfect" child. Responsibility is really just the ability to respond to situations and to learn from them.

> Responsibility is really just the ability to respond to situations and to learn from them.

ADAPTABILITY

THE THIRD SYSTEMIC SKILL, ADAPTABILITY, is among the strongest survival capabilities of the human race. This skill tends to be overlooked in our age of specialization, when we are increasingly preoccupied with finding the "real me." At the height of the Me Generation, the prevailing notion seemed to be that the main goal in life is to find oneself as if somewhere beyond easy grasp lies the valid self of each person, waiting to be found. In reality, each human being is a multiplicity of selves and thus as multifaceted as a diamond. And each facet of each person is valid in some contexts and invalid in others. The sooner we learn to accept and integrate our multiple identities, the closer we come to maturity.

Maturity is that point in life at which we can creatively manage our own multiplicity. By this time, we have learned the skill of *adaptability,* which means we can choose the facet of our personality that is appropriate to the particular time in question. Immature people erroneously believe that they have a single-faceted personality that applies to all situations. Thus, they ignore feedback, fail to anticipate the consequences of their behavior, and never learn how to adapt effectively without unnecessarily compromising. A typical comment expressing this limitation is "That's just the way I am." The mature person, on the other hand, changes somewhat with the environment, is alert to feedback regarding his or her personality and responds to it, and knows how to adapt to unexpected situations. This adaptability allows the mature human being to feel at home under most circumstances.

> The mature person changes somewhat with the environment, is alert to feedback regarding his or her personality and responds to it, and knows how to adapt to unexpected situations.

Let's take a closer look at the ability to adapt. At this moment Steve exists in myriad forms: husband, father, friend, counselor, coach, lover, child, and many more. Each identity is legitimately Steve, and each is appropriate in one context and inappropriate in another.

Suppose Steve has been away on a trip. All week he has been a lecturer, counselor, consultant, and psychologist. Even though he has watched his funds closely, he flies home in the evening nearly bankrupt. He discovers that he has just enough money, if he shakes his pockets, to pay the parking ransom on his car and head for home. The airline food wasn't that good, so he is still hungry. He passes the golden arches and has a Big Mac attack but does not have enough money to respond. It is approaching the end of the month. He has all the bills from the trip plus many others to pay. By the time he reaches home, the accountant facet of Steve's personality is ruminating over all the financial challenges he faces.

It is late in the evening when Steve drives into the garage. As he approaches the front door of the house and reaches for it, it opens. He sees the flickering of candles on the wall. He hears the easy-listening radio station that he likes best. As he is about to step into the doorway, a lovely person in a new negligee steps out from behind the door to greet him.

At that exact moment, if the accountant is still holding sway, Steve is in deep difficulty, for he would undoubtedly have to say, "How much did that cost? What's the matter, did they cut off the electricity?" The repercussions of that kind of response at such a time could echo throughout Steve's marriage for years.

But Steve is a mature person and therefore reads the situation and asks himself, "Which outcome do I most desire at this moment? If I want to criticize my wife and grumpily strut my stuff as an accountant, I could do that. On the other hand, if I acknowledge that she has gone out of her way to let me know it was not the accountant she missed most this trip, I can select another aspect of myself that would be more appropriate to this situation. I could say to the accountant, 'Get lost for a while,' and pull out lover, friend, responder, and warm human being."

So Steve has a choice. On the one hand, he can choose to adapt successfully to the situation at hand both to affirm his wife's efforts and to go after what he himself would like best to get out of that moment. Or he can choose the pseudo-"real" Steve, responding with "Hey, don't give me this crap. I'm broke." The latter, of course, would be inappropriate, irresponsible, and hurtful to his wife. And it would be certain to have a negative effect on the marriage.

Now, suppose that on the next weekend, in anticipation of repeating another romantic welcome, Steve finds himself running through the airport, leaping the turnstile, leaving his bag behind to be claimed on another day, ignoring the golden arches, whipping home ready for love, finally facing a closed door that doesn't open by itself. Once he gets out his key and unlocks it, he finds the lights all shining brightly. As he enters the room, his potential friend and lover is down on her knees, in jeans, scrubbing up a mess left by a sick child. In that moment if he chooses to pat her on the backside and say, "Hey, I'm ready for love," he would probably find himself wearing the towel on his head. Obviously, this is the moment to say to the lover within himself, "You had better get lost for a while." At this time it is more appropriate to become a helpmate and friend and say, "Wow, honey, it looks like you've had a hell of a night. What can I do to help you out?" That response would indicate a mature ability to consider a situation and adapt to it effectively. Many young people have a very limited repertoire of options and have not learned to adapt in this way, so they apply inappropriate aspects of themselves to situations and endlessly complicate their lives.

> Many young people have a very limited repertoire of options and have not learned to adapt, so they apply inappropriate aspects of themselves to situations and endlessly complicate their lives.

FLEXIBILITY

THE PALM TREE HAS THE FLEXIBILITY to bend with the wind. When it bends, does it remain laid over? No. It bends with a wind that is strong enough to tear its roots out if it remains rigid, but when the wind dies down, it straightens up again.

Flexibility is the ability to bend when we find ourselves in unworkable positions. A universal characteristic of insanity is inflexibly, doing the same thing over and over while hoping for different results. Flexibility in the face of changing circumstances, by contrast, is a hallmark of mental health.

BARRIERS TO THE DEVELOPMENT OF SYSTEMIC SKILLS

BOTH STRICTNESS AND PERMISSIVENESS, AS outlined in chapter 6, discourage the development of systemic skills and should be avoided in child raising.

Strictness

Strictness, the excessive imposition of power, usually involves some type of threat and requires children to learn to comply or rebel rather than to think and respond. Elsewhere, we point out that one drawback of control based on reward and punishment is that it limits people to a relatively low level of human understanding, one based on stimulus/response alone. A child operating on such a level can conceive of only two options: to obey or to rebel.

> *Flexibility is the ability to bend when we find ourselves in unworkable positions.*

An understanding of the developmental process can help us understand why spanking, although hardly ever the most effective teaching tool, can seem effective for children between the ages of two and six. Children are then at this stimulus/response level of understanding, and they do not think about the spanking so much as they respond to it directly. However, when children mature into perceptual human beings, they begin to think about punishment after their initial reaction. The "Three R's of Punishment" (see the sidebar on the next page) reflect the range of thinking that people engage in following punishment.

Many adults have a false perception about the effectiveness of punishment because it seems to work; it momentarily stops the misbehavior. However, when we look at the negative long-range results shown in the Three R's of Punishment, it is obvious we need to use better means to teach children how

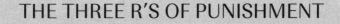

THE THREE R'S OF PUNISHMENT

1. *Resentment:* "This is unfair. I can't trust adults."

2. *Revenge:* "They are winning now, but I'll get even."

3. *Retreat, in one of three extremes:*

    a. *Rebellion:* "I'll do what I want and just be more careful not to get caught next time. I have a right to lie and cheat under these circumstances."

    b. *Reduced self-esteem:* "I must really be a bad person who deserves to be punished. I will keep trying to please, but I'm not much good at it."

    c. *Retirement:* "I give up. I can't win, so why try? I wish people would just leave me alone."

their behavior and its results interrelate. We need to help them understand the systemic principle of cause and effect.

Permissiveness

Permissiveness shields the child from experiencing the consequences of his or her actions. In this case, both parent and child abdicate responsibility. Children learn to use their energy and intelligence to manipulate the parents into rescuing and protecting them from the consequences and results of their behavior. But the long-range results can be devastating when children find that they cannot manipulate other people the way they did their parents. Such a rude awakening often results in a life of frustration, anger, or depression. Even worse, some become so effective as manipulators that they do succeed in making others do their bidding. They become users who believe that, since they can usually escape consequences, their end justifies any means to attain what they want.

Parents are often permissive because being so is easier than imposing limits. But the long-range results of their permissiveness can complicate their

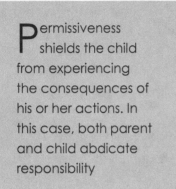

Permissiveness shields the child from experiencing the consequences of his or her actions. In this case, both parent and child abdicate responsibility

lives when they discover that as the children get older, meeting their ever-growing needs becomes harder. In especially permissive homes, where children believe that the world owes them a living, they ask to be bailed out of the problems they themselves create. Such behavior denies the truth of cause and effect.

THE BUILDERS OF SYSTEMIC SKILLS

THERE ARE THREE ELEMENTS TO the teaching of responsibility and the other systemic skills:

1. *Unqualified positive regard, love, and respect.* Unqualified positive regard is possible only when we understand and acknowledge that children differ in their perceptions, learning styles, and developmental levels.

2. *Clear feedback about behavior.* We must reinforce our children's acceptable behavior and accomplishment with specific recognition and appreciation and avoid generic praise. Conversely, we must give specific feedback for unacceptable behavior and avoid generic criticism.

3. *A consequential environment.* We create a consequential environment when we follow up our agreed-on decisions with firmness, dignity, and respect. Pointing up the natural and logical consequences of actions through the EIAG method is an excellent way to foster the development of children's systemic skills.

Natural Consequences

Consequences happen naturally as the result of certain choices or behaviors. For example, when we go out in the rain without a raincoat, we get wet. If we forget to take a lunch, we go hungry. As noted throughout this book, children learn a great deal when we allow them to experience natural consequences without interference.

If a child loses her baseball mitt, the natural consequence would be for her to live without a baseball mitt. However, most parents cannot stand to see their little darlings do without, especially if this means they might miss a Little League game. That attitude would be fine if these parents would tell the truth and simply say, "I can't stand to see you miss the game, so you don't have to be responsible. Any time you lose your mitt, I will rush out and buy you a new one." Instead, the conversation goes more like this: "How many times have I told you to take care of your mitt? If you were more responsible, this would not happen. When will you ever learn?" The lecture goes on while the parent is out helping the child look for her mitt. The parent usually tells the ultimate lie on the way to the store to buy a new mitt: "This is absolutely the last time I will buy you a new mitt." Both know this is not the last time. All the child needs to do to get a new mitt is to lose the one currently in hand.

A better response from the parent would be "Gee, honey, I'm sorry you lost your mitt. That must be very disappointing." No matter how much the child begs and cries for a new mitt, the subject would be closed. Children are much less likely to be irresponsible when they have to experience such natural consequences of their own behavior.

However, sometimes a parent must suspend the lesson of natural consequences. One should never employ natural consequences under the following circumstances:

1. *When there is immediate danger to the child.* For example, never allow the child to experience the natural consequences of running into a busy intersection.

2. *When there is immediate danger to another person or to property.* Never allow a child to experience the natural consequences of throwing a rock at someone or through a window. In both of these cases it is best, as Rudolph Dreikurs put it, "to shut your mouth and act." Teaching can come later, when a climate of support has been established.

3. *When future consequences are at stake.* For example, never allow a child to experience the natural consequences of eating poorly or foregoing oral hygiene.

4. *When a child is not old enough to understand how to prevent the natural consequence.* A two-year-old cannot be expected to remember his or her lunch for preschool.

> A spanking is not logically related to any behavior. Nor is spanking respectful—it is hurtful and humiliating.

THE THREE R'S OF LOGICAL CONSEQUENCES

1. *Related* to the behavior
2. *Respectful* to both child and adult
3. *Reasonable* to both child and adult

5. *When adults cannot keep their mouths shut.* The benefits of a natural consequence are canceled out when adults add their comments to the consequences. If a child is going hungry as a natural consequence of forgetting his or her lunch, the child is likely to think about how to avoid this experience in the future and could be in the process of learning internal locus of control. If an adult intervenes with "That's what you get for being irresponsible. How many times do I have to remind you? Maybe next time you'll remember," the child's attention is more likely to focus on the "mean old adult," which could reinforce development of an external locus of control.

After a cooling-off period following the natural consequences, use the EIAG process to check on the child's conclusions regarding the experience and to help him or her achieve appropriate conclusions where the reasoning has gone awry.

Logical Consequences

Logical consequences do not happen naturally; they are set up by adults or children. This would be an appropriate logical consequence in our baseball mitt example: "I'll be happy to take you to the store to buy a new mitt if you have saved enough money from your allowance to pay for it or if you would like the money to be deducted from your allowance. However, I have a very busy schedule today, and going to the store will take about half an hour. As soon as you have helped me accomplish one of my chores, we'll leave. Which would you like to do—weed for half an hour or wash my car?" By the way, giving in to the child's promise to complete the chore "later" is an invitation to a power struggle.

Many parents have asked us, "Well, if my child knows in advance that he is going to get a spanking, isn't that a logical consequence?" The answer is no. A consequence is not logical if it is lacking in any of the following Three R's of Logical Consequences:

1. *Related* to the behavior
2. *Respectful* to both child and adult
3. *Reasonable* to both child and adult

A spanking is not logically related to any behavior. Nor is spanking respectful—it is hurtful and humiliating. And, although many adults think spanking is reasonable, you won't find many children who agree. There was a time in our developmental level as a species when spanking was effective. However, the more intelligent we become as a species, the less effective spanking is.

Another common question is this: "What about the next two popular methods for discipline today—grounding and removal of privileges? Are they logical consequences?" The answer is yes and no.

One of the biggest mistakes parents make is trying to disguise punishment by calling it a logical consequence. The feelings behind what we do are more important than what we do, because they determine our attitude, our tone of voice, and the way our children perceive our actions. Unfortunately, some adults are more interested in making children "pay" for what they have done than in using the most effective ways to help children correct their behavior.

Let's evaluate grounding with respect to this criterion. Over the long term, grounding is an ineffective punishment when it is used for revenge, to make children suffer, to show them who is boss, or because the parent doesn't know what else to do. But grounding can be effective when it is directly related to the misbehavior in question, when it is administered in a respectful manner, and when it is reasonable.

Consider the language here: "I don't want to hear your excuses. Get to your room and think about the terrible thing you did. I don't understand how you could have done such a thing. I can't tell you how disappointed I am in you." In this case grounding is designed to put the child down rather than to inspire improvement in his or her behavior. We can, therefore, expect this punishment to be ineffective over the long haul.

> Logical consequences are reasonable when they are agreed on in advance by adults and children together.

In contrast, an effective grounding might be administered like this: "We all make mistakes. Go to your room until you feel better and then we will work out a solution." Here the grounding is intended to create a cooling-off period so that a climate of support can arise in which improvement in small steps can take place.

Logical consequences are reasonable when they are agreed on in advance by adults and children together. To ground a child to positive effect, it is a good idea to discuss the possible grounding in advance. Let the child know that the purpose is not humiliation or suffering but rather to give everyone involved a chance to calm down. It would be valid to suggest, in such a case, that while the child is grounded at home, he or she might want to read, listen to music, take a nap, or play some games. Some adults see encouraging such pastimes as rewarding negative behavior. But they are under the mistaken impression that children will not do better until after they feel worse. In fact, making children feel worse creates a threatening environment in which no constructive learning can take place. But making them feel better and leaving it at that is not recommended, either. It is important to follow up and work on solutions when everyone is feeling good and is, therefore, receptive. The point here is to start from a climate of support and then work on constructive consequences.

After children have experienced a consequence consistent with the Three R's of Logical Consequences, they usually feel that they have been treated fairly and responsibly even if they are unhappy. However, poorly administered punishment, even if it seems to eliminate the misbehavior, usually leaves them with the negative feelings outlined earlier in the Three R's of Punishment.

WHEN THE CHILD COMES HOME LATE: AN EXAMPLE

WHAT USUALLY HAPPENS WHEN A child who agreed to be home at midnight doesn't show up? By 12:30 most parents are assuming the worst: raped, killed, run off, kidnapped, eloped, crashed. By 1:30 they are at their wit's end. Then the child shows up suddenly, fully intact, and the parents are livid with rage at the evidence of the child's very survival. What prompted all that concern? Love. What do we give the child when he or she gets home? Fury.

Let's look at what a mature parent would say to the late arrival: "Son, I'm glad you're home. I was beginning to think of the terrible things that might have happened to you, and I got in touch with how much I love you. We will talk in the morning about what this will mean for the rest of the month."

Now, what would this boy assume in the absence of data about the consequences he will reap? He assumes the worst: grounded forever, no prom, no car. By 5:00 A.M. he will be in the parents' bedroom crying, "Is it morning yet, Dad?"

"No, still sleeping in here."

He'll be back again at 7:00. "Are you ready yet?"

"No, I'm sleeping in this morning."

The Child's Age

Age is an important consideration in determining logical consequences. Logical consequences for children up to three years old are rarely effective. At this age it is more appropriate to use supervision, distraction, and redirection or to decide what you will do and use action instead of words. For example, when a child is having a temper tantrum in a grocery store, kindly and firmly take the child to the car and read a book until she is finish having her feelings and then ask whether she is ready to try again. This usually won't take longer than five to ten minutes. For three- to six-year-old children, a consequence (lost privilege) should last no more than one hour. Consequences for children six to eight years of age should last no longer than one day. For children from eight to twelve a week is plenty, and for ages twelve through eighteen, consequences should be limited to the amount of time it takes for the child to come up with a solution to the problem.

> In setting up consequences, the point is to squeeze the children enough to get their attention but inspire them enough to promote positive change.

Consequences that exceed these time limits are likely to seem like consecutive life sentences. They destroy the child's incentive to improve. In setting up consequences, the point is to squeeze the children enough to get their attention but inspire them enough to promote positive change. Any plan that goes beyond that point amounts to punishment to get even. Where that is the case,

children will then get even with us by refusing to grow up and by learning to dodge us whenever they can.

Steve's two neighbors provide examples of extremes involving age readiness for logical consequences. One neighbor used the belt on his five-year-old in anger. The child could think of nothing but the pain of that beating and afterward felt hurt and resentful. The other neighbor said to his five-year-old, "Honey, given the existential reality of our relationship and our need to be mellow and affirming together, I mean, like if it wouldn't bum you out too much . . . ," and that child was totally bewildered. In both cases the parent's "rhetoric" was inappropriate for the level of the five-year-old.

Here's a statement a five-year-old can understand: "Honey, it is a rule in our family that we don't take plates of food into the family room. From now on you will need to eat at the table." If the child then breaks the rule, it will be ineffective to say, "How many times do I have to tell you . . . ?" Effective follow-up would be "Honey, what is our rule?" After about thirty or forty times, the five-year-old will begin to understand. But now when your five-year-old sees you heading for the family room with food, he's sure to say, "It is a rule in this family that we don't take food into the family room." Beware of children's clarity at this age!

Children will operate at this level until about age seven or eight, when they will begin to ask such questions as "Why is that a rule in this family?" This is not the time to say, "Because I said so." At this age children are not testing you with their questions; they are trying to substitute insight and understanding for conditioned behavior—to make the jump to conventional reasoning.

A wise parent would answer such questions this way: "Honey, I made that rule when you were little because we had some nice furniture in the family room, and I was trying to protect it. Now, what rules can you think of to help me protect what we have left?"

By getting children involved at this level, you might find that they do come up with some rules. They will consider your invitation a vote of confidence and an acknowledgment of their increasing maturity. But don't go too far. When children reach age eleven, it is inappropriate to say, "Hey, if you are going to hassle me, stay out as long as you want. We'll see you around over the weekend." This attitude gives too much latitude. Rather, at this age, children can understand this kind of statement: "Under normal circumstances you should plan on 10:30 P.M. for your curfew. That doesn't mean you can't ever do anything after that time, but it means you shouldn't plan on it. Come and talk with me if there is something special, and I will consider it."

It is important that your rules evolve to fit the age group. Avoid saying to a seventeen-year-old, "You know your curfew is always 11:00 P.M. We already discussed this three years ago." Such a remark is likely to encourage kids to drive 100 miles an hour so they can sneak in under the wire on the night it is their turn to drop everybody off. Those same kids, if they don't get killed trying to make their curfew, will later go away to college or work and possibly self-destruct in the face of the freedom they have never been taught to handle. The family will consider college to have destroyed them, when in reality the destructive factor will have been the parents' failure to anticipate the child's need for increased freedom and flexibility along with increased responsibility and self-discipline.

> Whenever possible, involve young people in setting up logical consequences. They grasp the Three R's of Logical Consequences very quickly from the age of four years old.

To seventeen-year-olds the appropriate message is this: "We need to go over what you plan to do so we can agree on a reasonable time to expect you home. Once the limit is set, it is your responsibility to respect the decision. By keeping our agreed-on commitments, you demonstrate that you are responsible enough to supervise yourself."

By the way, logical consequences do not have to be expressed verbally and can be administered to children at a very young age. A toddler who fools with the television can be put into a playpen without a word or cross look and then taken out in five minutes. Once he or she touches the television again, it's back into the playpen for another short stint. It won't take too long for very young children to understand that they had better stay away from the television if they want to stay out of the playpen.

The Cooling-Off Period

Mature parents refuse to deal with the most important people in their lives when they are at their worst. When parents are coming down from the peak of fear, chances are that all they'd be able to do is make idiots of themselves. It's certainly no time to reason out the consequences of a serious infraction of family rules.

Steve's daughter was once asked, "What is the hardest thing about dealing with your dad?"

She said, "When I make a mistake, he's quiet, and he respects me. That way I know I have a problem. It was a lot nicer when he used to yell and scream and make an ass of himself. Then I knew he had a problem."

Whenever children sense our anger coming toward them, they consider the anger and not what they did to cause it as the cause of their problems. If we can keep our dignity and allow them theirs, we are much more likely to cause change in behavior.

GETTING CHILDREN INVOLVED

WHENEVER POSSIBLE, INVOLVE YOUNG PEOPLE in setting up logical consequences. They grasp the Three R's of Logical Consequences very quickly from the age of four years old. Family meetings are an excellent time to work out such consequences. Once agreement has been reached, get the terms clear while the atmosphere of cooperation prevails. Don't say, "If you don't do it, you will suffer." Be clear on exactly what the suffering will be, for how long, and under what circumstances. Finally, avoid saying, "Do you understand?"

Use dialogue to clarify the agreement: "What is your understanding of what will happen if you don't pick up your toys?" Older children are capable of understanding a longer series of questions: "What is your understanding of the time you must be home? What is your understanding of what will happen if you are not home at that time? Who will decide whether you continue to go out? How will you make that decision tonight?"

Firmness

When follow-through is required, it is important to be firm. As we have emphasized throughout this book, it is important to live up to our promises. We should love our children enough to say what we mean and mean what we say—and be willing to run the risk of their temporary displeasure with firm follow-through. Research shows that the children of parents who do not set up logical consequences or who do not follow through on those consequences they set believe their parents do not love them. Children whose parents are too strict or arbitrary have the same problem because they are not afforded dignity or respect.

> We should love our children enough to say what we mean and mean what we say—and be willing to run the risk of their temporary displeasure with firm follow-through.

Dignity

Dignity means following through on agreements without directing anger at the child. Human beings go through a strange metamorphosis when they feel anger directed toward them; they believe their problems are due to the anger rather than their actions. The drunk who comes home to a furious wife goes to bed secure, saying, "No wonder I drink, with an unreasonable old bag like that waiting for me at home."

Respect

We demonstrate our respect for others primarily through our attitudes and tone of voice. Respect begins with the belief that children create their own difficulties without additional help from us. Once we have placed privileges and responsibilities in their hands, we need to respect what they do with them and avoid trying to get even with them because we are upset about the consequences.

This is the language of respect: "Son, I am sorry you decided to handle it this way, but I have to respect the decision you just made to cancel your plans for the rest of the month." Simply taking something away from children to punish them for misbehavior creates resistance; children see such an action as unfair and unrelated to their own actions.

MANIPULATION

YOUNG PEOPLE ARE FAMOUS FOR trying to manipulate parents into canceling consequences: "But, Dad, there was this seven-foot caterpillar crawling across the interstate and all the phone booths were filled with winos and derelicts." When confronted with such an off-the-wall comment, we can step back quickly and let it hit the other wall without getting involved. No grown person of sound mind should stand around at 1:00 o'clock in the morning lobbying for his or her position in the face of such nonsense.

It is important to consider possible extenuating circumstances fairly; however, accepting or getting involved with unreasonable, invalid, or unsound excuses is self-defeating.

A SUMMARY

THE TEACHING OF THE SYSTEMIC skills, particularly responsibility, produces great challenges and pressures for most families. Here is a summary of the steps involved:

1. *Avoid strictness* (excessive control).
2. *Avoid permissiveness* (excessive autonomy, too little structure and follow-through).
3. *Convey unqualified love, care, and respect* (distinguish action from people and avoid using love, praise, and approval as rewards).
4. *Give clear feedback* ("I feel . . . about . . . because . . .").

5. *Structure consequences* (teach children the relationship between cause and effect—for example, responsibilities and privileges).

6. *Be firm* (say what you mean and mean what you say).

7. *Maintain dignity* (avoid projecting anger or other feelings onto the child; be an actor rather than a reactor; choose to deal with things when you are at your best rather than at your worst).

8. *Teach with respect* (clarify what they have caused to happen rather than what you have done to punish them).

Successful application of these principles promotes responsibility, adaptability, and flexibility. It also contributes to maturity in judgment, which we will explore in the next chapter.

10

Fostering Strong Judgmental Skills

JUDGEMENT REQUIRES THE application of abstract ideas to real life. The seventh principle of the Significant Seven helps children develop strong judgmental skills. It gives them the ability to assess a situation with respect to its practical and ethical appropriateness and to make decisions on the basis of that assessment.

A U.S. Air Force training manual describes *decision making* as "handling an incident" and *judgment* as "bringing in higher-order considerations." Often in life we can make several possible choices to handle a given situation. This is part of decision making. When we learn to ask ourselves what other issues might be involved and how the options influence them, we are exercising judgment. For example: "What is the fairest and most respectful way to handle this?" brings moral and ethical considerations into the mix.

> Judgment is a learned skill, and there is only one way to develop it: to practice.

Judgment is a learned skill, and there is only one way to develop it: to practice. The available evidence indicates that moral and ethical development requires a mentorship process between children/youth and more mature individuals. Tragically, many parents believe that judgment is like sex: Children are born with it but should not practice it for a long, long time.

BARRIERS TO THE DEVELOPMENT OF JUDGMENT

UNFORTUNATELY, OUR COMPLEX WORLD CONTAINS several obstacles to developing mature judgment.

Barrier 1: Unaware Parents

Parents find it easier and more expedient to lecture, instruct, explain, moralize, and ultimately make all judgments themselves than to encourage children to think through an issue or an event. Such adults retard the development of judgmental maturity and critical thinking, inhibit the acquisition of wisdom, and replace them with threat and intimidation.

Barrier 2: Naive Peers

By the time children go to school, peers are often their primary source of learning and experience. But when this is the case, judgmental development is often retarded, because peer means "same level of insight, awareness, and understanding." When children have dialogue primarily with peers, they fail to be exposed to those with more advanced insights and more highly developed faculties. In the traditional family, now a distinct minority, interaction with siblings was important to the developmental process, as was time spent with grandparents and parents. In addition, in past generations children spent little time with peers and most of their time with siblings or extended family members. Thus, they got constant practice in assessment and judgment. Our children, who are constantly engrossed in peer-centered activities, interact minimally with those more mature than themselves.

Barrier 3: A Failure to Allow for Developmental Stages

In the previous chapter, we discussed developmental readiness, an important factor to consider in helping children develop the Significant Seven perceptions, capabilities, and skills. With respect to judgment and reasoning skills, people go through fairly predictable stages in their development. Parents need to recognize and allow for the basic stages of cognitive development, which influence the emergence of judgmental skills. The following story illustrates this.

Terry was an extremely bright two-year-old. One Saturday evening he attended a drive-in movie with his parents. Two weeks later he was riding in the car with his father when they passed the same drive-in theater. Terry recognized it and commented, "We went there last night." His father stopped the car and gave Terry a spanking for lying. This father did not understand cognitive development. Terry showed highly developed perceptive skills in recognizing the location of the theater two weeks after he had been there, but he had not yet developed a clear understanding of time and did not have the cognitive maturity to understand the difference between last night and two weeks ago. He was not lying.

> Using judgment and controlling one's own behavior require the ability to anticipate future consequences of present behavior. This in turn depends on the ability to focus attention, understand causal relationships, and anticipate future events—all skills that develop with age.

Using judgment and controlling one's own behavior require the ability to anticipate future consequences of present behavior. This in turn depends on the ability to focus attention, understand causal relationships, and anticipate future events—all skills that develop with age. It is important to note that the Swiss psychologist Jean Piaget discovered that children are not capable of abstract thinking (judgment) during the early years and that the process of developing judgment is also a developmental issue.[1]

For example, suppose we give a two-year-old the choice of a candy bar in one hand and a $100 bill in the other hand. The child will take the candy every time. Give an eight-year-old the same choice, and the $100 bill will win every time. If we ask the two-year-old to explain choosing the candy, he or she won't even understand the question. But the eight-year-old will quickly tell us that $100 will buy many, many candy bars. This child has acquired an ability to focus on an abstract question and bring to bear a knowledge of cause and effect on its solution.

---

1. For more information on the developmntal process, see *Positive Discipline: The First Three Years* and *Positive Discipline for Preschoolers* by Jane Nelsen, Cheryl Erwin, and Roslyn Duffy.

Parents must learn when children are ready to use judgment. Some parents think they must spank two-year-olds to teach them not to run into the street. They don't seem to realize that two-year-olds lack the necessary maturity to judge safety no matter how many spankings they receive. In such muddled cases, the spanking is for the parents' benefit, not the child's.

A two-year-old also does not understand "no" the way some parents may believe. "No" is an abstract concept. Therefore, it is not effective to spank young children to teach them "judgment" about running into the street. It is effective, however, to let a young child practice judgment about crossing the street with your close supervision.

A responsible parent will physically restrain a small child from running into the street while taking every opportunity to engage the child in dialogue when the child is ready: "What do we need to watch for before we cross the street? How many ways do we need to look before we know it is safe? What might happen if we don't look both ways?" So, even though you are practicing, you would not let children cross a street by themselves until they are around the age of eight.

Table 10.1 traces developmental stages by age as discerned by pioneering psychologists Piaget and Lawrence Kohlberg. Use this table to guide you in assessing your child's judgmental maturity.

Table 10.1   The Development of Judgment by Age

Age	Type of Thinking	Judgment Types-Principles
0–2	Sensorimotor	World of here and now
		Pain/pleasure Can/can't
2–6	Preoperational	Sees only one aspect at a time
		Thinking is rigid
		Black/white
		Safe/dangerous

Table 10.1   The Development of Judgment by Age (continued)

Age	Type of Thinking	Judgment Types-Principles
6–11	Concrete	Begins to under-stand relationships
		Able to use logical thought only when solv-ing problems involving concrete objects and events
11+	Abstract	Cause and effect
		Legal/illegal
		What will happen if . . . ?
		Capable of dealing with the hypothetical
		Discriminates abstract concepts
		Appropriate/inappropriate
		Fair/unfair
		How will . . . feel about . . . ?

In a fun and challenging book *The Rise and Fall of the American Teenager,* Thomas Hines documents the emergence of the concept of "teenager" as we currently use it in the United States. He makes the point that much of what we view as "normal adolescent behavior" is actually deviant behavior by world and historic standards. It appears to be a result of our radically changed lifestyle; a number of rather unfortunate assumptions made about raising and educat-ing children in the postwar era; a modern, consumer society without clearly defined roles for young people; and the erosion of cultural norms, boundaries, rites of passage, and support with respect to young people.

Historically, adolescence has always been seen as a time of great change and adaptation to adult roles. However, the word *teenager* was rarely used until the mid-1950s. When children were needed for economic survival, they were given so much responsibility that by the age of twelve, they often had the same judgmental skills as most adults. They were not as greatly influenced by peers as children are today, and they were free from the endless entertainment options of our overindulgent age. And, although they had to deal with the new feelings and emotions of puberty, as children do today, they did so in a more stable environment.

Today, of course, adolescents are at greater risk of being drawn into trouble. We might even hypothesize that they need sharper skills of judgment than children of less dangerous times. Parents certainly recognize this need, but too often they fail to understand their adolescents' developmental readiness and insight level. These parents are likely to feel inadequate as child rearers and to use adultisms. Such treatment only increases feelings of inadequacy in teenagers and encourages them to seek meaning, purpose, and relevance among their peers.

LOSING GAINS DURING ADOLESCENCE

MANY ELEMENTARY SCHOOLS TODAY OFFER excellent substance abuse education programs. It is not unusual to hear a ten- or eleven-year-old say with great clarity, "I will never be dumb enough to smoke or drink or use drugs. I don't want to do that to my body." Parents often give a sigh of relief when they hear this, believing they can relax and trust their children's judgment forevermore. When these same kids reach thirteen and fourteen years of age and start staying out late or coming home stoned, their parents become confused and often feel that they have failed. They may try excessive control and punishment out of fear, which usually increases rebellion in teens. Alternatively, they try to deny that a problem exists, because "my child said he would never do such a thing." At this point, a good grounding in the developmental stages of adolescence can decrease the confusion and guide parents in their actions.

As young people progress through their stages, they are even more in need of experience and practice in developing the Significant Seven concepts. They need to know that their parents understand their feelings but also understand

DEVELOPMENTAL STAGES IN ADOLESCENCE

The following are guidelines to the developmental stages that occur during adolescence:

Early Adolescence (12 to 14 years)

1. Begin questioning parent's values
2. Are often moody
3. Form close friendships; would rather go out with their friends than parents
4. Realize parents aren't perfect; identify their faults
5. Follow interests and clothing styles of peer groups

Middle Adolescence (14 to 17 years)

1. Become self-involved, alternating between unrealistically inflated self-concepts and poor self-concepts
2. Complain that parents interfere with their independence
3. Are intensely concerned with appearance and bodies; are beginning to primp and strut
4. Have a diminished opinion of parents; withdraw emotionally from them; draw a sense of identity from peer group

Late Adolescence (17 to 19 years)

1. Have firmer identities
2. Are better at expressing feelings in words
3. Have a more developed sense of humor
4. Are more emotionally stable, with fewer mood swings than at earlier stages
5. Take more pride in their work; are more self-reliant

the dangers they are facing. They need the security of parents who will continue to offer firm limits with dignity and respect and out of love and concern. Family traditions and family meetings, imbued with support, are more critical than ever. More than ever, adults may need to make more conscious efforts to encourage the development of judgmental skills in order for children to thrive in modern society.

BUILDERS FOR DEVELOPING JUDGMENT

HERE ARE SOME POSITIVE STEPS parents can take to help children improve their judgmental skills.

Builder 1: Dialogue and Collaboration

For years we assumed that the developmental stages previously outlined occur automatically. Now we know that children need practice and experience to progress through these stages.

The old farmer, in the world of yesterday, realized the importance of teaching his son about the family business. He knew that if anything happened to him, the survival of his family ultimately depended on his son's good judgment. He realized that at some point he would have to stop directing—"It is time to cut the hay"—and say to his son, "If you had to decide whether we cut the hay or not today, what would you look for? What do you think?" He would listen to his son's response—"I think we should cut it, Dad"—and then check further: "Well, what about that thunderhead coming over the mountain?"

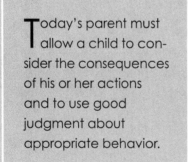

Today's parent must allow a child to consider the consequences of his or her actions and to use good judgment about appropriate behavior.

"Gee, I didn't look at the sky. I was looking at the grass, Dad."

"Well, what will happen if you get all this hay cut and then that thunderhead brings a big rain?"

"It will ruin all the hay."

In that way, following the tried-and-true apprenticeship model, the father challenged the son to develop his judgmental skills. Ultimately, the apprentice had to make his own decisions—select some lumber, make the first cut, and so on—but how could he do that without being allowed to plunge ahead and risk error? In a similar vein, today's parent must allow a child to consider the consequences of his or her actions and to use good judgment about appropriate behavior.

> Role taking is effective only when adults have the patience and courage to allow their children to go at their own paces and make their own mistakes.

Builder 2: Provide Role-Taking Opportunities

Role taking occurs when we place children in the role of the decision-maker and let them attempt to apply their knowledge, experience, and insight to an actual or hypothetical situation. Role taking, first described by Lawrence Kohlberg in his studies of cognitive and moral development, is an apprenticeship in thinking and discovering wisdom.

Judgmental skills develop when parents, teachers, and other adults create or allow children to become involved in situations from which they cannot escape except through thinking. Role taking is effective only when adults have the patience and courage to allow their children to go at their own paces and make their own mistakes (discussed further in the next section). You can help your children develop their judgmental skills by providing role-taking experiences for them as early as possible. For example, ask them, "If you had to make this decision, what things would you need to consider?" or "If you were in my situation, what kinds of problems or concerns might you have about deciding what to do?"

Notice that we did not say, "What would you do?" We said, "What would you need to find out, learn, allow for, take into consideration?" and so forth. However, as a general rule, allow young people to act as decision-makers with things that are safe for them to handle and that can inconvenience them but not impair them. Then resolve to be willing to accept the children's choices and coach them when their choices don't work out well.

Recently, Steve saw the role-taking process played out very poorly. He was at a shoe store and heard a parent say, "You can choose your new shoes." The boy immediately went for an expensive pair of cowboy boots. The mother said, "I didn't mean those," instantly doubting the child's judgment. Then, irritated, she walked over and grabbed two pairs of tennis shoes on sale, plunked them down, and said, "Choose one of these."

Steve's ten-year-old son, standing beside him said, "Dad, he won't wear either pair." Family closets are filled with things that should be taken to Goodwill because parents bought them for practical reasons when their children had chosen something else. Children get even by ignoring the things their parents have chosen.

This mother could have said, "I have set aside $15 to get you some shoes. You may go through the store and choose the pair you want for that amount or less. You will have to get by with whatever you choose for three months until I can afford to replace them."

As Steve left the shoe store, he heard another mother say to a child, "You can choose where we have lunch." The child chose a fast-food place. The mother immediately came back with "But, honey, they have such a nice salad bar at this other restaurant." The child said, "But I want to go here."

Said the mother, "You know I like salad at this time of the day." She was already manipulating, pulling the rug out from under the child. This incident will teach the child to avoid making choices and to have less confidence in the ones she does make.

Builder 3: Provide Opportunities for Children to Experience the Consequences of Their Choices

We help young people develop judgment when we are willing to allow them to make mistakes, experience the consequences of making a poor choice, and let them live with their decisions without bailing them out.

Steve and his wife had this experience with Kimbi, their style-conscious young daughter. They gave her a back-to-school clothes allotment. Kimbi rushed out and decided that instead of several interchangeable pieces of clothing, one Ralph Lauren original would be her sole purchase. The parents carefully explored the implications of that decision: "Honey, have you considered what kinds of things you will have to wear day in and day out?"

"Yes, I have, Dad. This is real neat and real important. This is what I want."

Then the adults asked, "Do you understand when your next school clothes allotment will come?" She verified that she understood it would be the following December and that it was now the beginning of September. That confirmed, she went ahead and bought her Ralph Lauren original.

Within a week she was bored stiff with the outfit, and her friends were even asking her if she washed it, at least. This touched off a great round of creativity. Having no budget, she took over some extra-large shirts that Steve had marginally worn out, got out the sewing machine, put in drawstrings, cut flaps, and added buttons to make coverlets and shields. Somehow, she made it until December. When she received her next school clothes allotment, she went out and bought several interchangeable outfits absent designer status to have a little more flexibility.

Parents are often afraid that by making poor decisions their children will lose their confidence and suffer low self-esteem. Actually, quite the contrary is true.

Steve and his wife would have canceled out a lot of important learning and validation if they had gone out and bought Kimbi a new wardrobe while pointing out the deficiencies in her judgment. In experiencing the consequences of a choice that, at worst, could only produce inconvenience and a little embarrassment, Kimbi became more confident and self-assured. When she went out to shop again, she showed better judgment and a clearer understanding of what she was doing. She is less likely in the future to go off half-cocked. Instead, she will ask, "What factors have I not considered?" Parents are often afraid that by making poor decisions their children will lose their confidence and suffer low self-esteem. Actually, quite the contrary is true. When young people discover that their choices affect outcomes, they feel potent and significant and become increasingly confident that they hold the reins in their lives. With practice, they become more adept in holding these reins—and better human beings.

Builder 4: Encourage Reflection on the What, Why, and How

The first requirement to making judgments is knowing how to analyze situations and which questions to ask to achieve insight. The what, why, and how of a situation constitute the basic material needed for making a judgment.

Children need help in learning what is significant in a situation, why it is significant, and how it could affect the outcome. Once they have made such an analysis, they can use their knowledge, insight, and experience to determine what to do about it. In summary, children need training in two stages of judgment: (1) analysis and (2) the application of ideas and wisdom. The ultimate result is a judgment.

Steve's son, Mike, approached him one evening with this remark: "Dad, Mom says you are going to be away for a couple of weeks. I was thinking, wouldn't it be nice if we went to the amusement park first as a sort of going-away celebration?"

"Son," Steve answered, "that sounds great." Then he decided use the opportunity do some training in judgmental skills: "It might be helpful to show you what I have to go through to decide whether we can go or not. First, I have to determine how much money we would need to go to the park. Why don't you come up with a list of the things we would need to spend money on? Then I'll estimate the cost of each and figure the total cost of the trip."

They estimated gas, admission, and food and came up with a budget of about $40. "The second thing I have to do," said Steve, "is look at what money we have on hand and what our priorities are at the present time." They were then building an addition on their home and had been cursed with good weather, so the contractors were running way ahead of schedule and squeezing the family for every dime. Steve went through the monthly expenses and came up with the balance, about $30.

Then, instead of making the ultimate decision for the boy, Steve said, "Son, since you know the cost of the trip and the amount of money on hand to use, what decision would you make if you were in my situation? Can we go on the trip?"

Mike looked it over and said, "Dad, I really don't think so. We're short $10."

"That's my conclusion, too," said Steve. "And while I really wish things were different, that's just the way it goes."

That night the boy came up to Steve and handed him $12.

"What's this?" said Steve.

"Sold some baseball cards," said the boy. "Now we can go to the park—and have two extra hot dogs, too!"

Did they go? Sure they did—with Steve feeling great about the boy's obvious growth and Mike feeling great about his impact.

PUTTING THE SIGNIFICANT SEVEN TOGETHER

WHAT DOES THE PRECEDING STORY demonstrate? In the context of the earlier chapters, it's a working demonstration of the Significant Seven:

1. Mike, at age ten, believes he is a capable person who can solve problems if he tries.

2. He believes he can contribute to a relationship that is important to him through his creativity, ideas, and resourcefulness.

3. He believes he can find a way to alter circumstances or his responses to them to influence his environment.

4. He shows some ability for self-assessment, self-control, and self-discipline.

5. He shows the ability to communicate, cooperate, negotiate, share, empathize, and listen.

6. He shows some understanding of limits and consequences, privileges and responsibilities, cause and effect, and his role in dealing with them.

7. He shows some ability to apply abstract notions—such as "can afford, can't afford"—in coming up with solutions to practical problems.

At age ten, Mike already believes he is capable, significant, and influential. He is developing the skills and capabilities that will enable him to be successful in anything he sets his mind to accomplish. He is showing problem-solving skills, initiative, creativity, and the ability to negotiate deals.

Did all that happen automatically? No. These skills and capabilities were the products of much time spent by his parents using the EIAG process, exploring rather than explaining, encouraging and inviting rather than directing, checking things out rather than assuming, celebrating Mike's accomplishments rather than deriding his mistakes, helping him see rather than requiring that he be a mind-reader, and showing respect instead of disgust for his behavior and opinions.

Mike is a capable young person developing maturity and good judgment. As the youngest in Steve's family, he has benefited from his parents' struggles with their older daughters and foster children as they learned to parent in a society lacking networks and other support systems.

LOVING SUPPORT WITHOUT RESCUING

ONE MORNING STEVE'S NINETEEN-YEAR-OLD DAUGHTER sat down on his bed, obviously wanting to talk. "What's up?" asked Steve.

"Oh, Dad, I don't know what to do. I have a good job offer, but I've also been accepted at college. I don't know which to choose."

Father and daughter discussed her perceptions of the relative strengths and weaknesses of each option. When they finished, she said, "What should I do, Daddy?"

Said Steve, "Honey, it's a decision only you can make."

"Dad, I've been making decisions my whole life," she said plaintively. "Couldn't you make just this one?"

With a full heart, Steve said, "Dear, I've learned that decisions are your life. I've seen you make some good ones and some not-so-good ones, but you've always learned from those you've made and have gone on with your life. This is a particularly important choice, and I love you too much to take it away from you."

"Oh, Daddy," she said, "I know you love me and that I have to choose. I guess I just needed to share some of the struggle with you."

The girl went on to make her choice, and she will choose again and again—for that is how capable people live.

11

A Blueprint for Success

ONE OF THE chief predictors of young people's success—regarding their performance, their motivation, their health, and their productivity—is their perception of their parents' image of them, not necessarily what parents believe about them but rather what they believe their parents believe about them. This distinction is important, and it has ramifications from earliest childhood.

Parents usually love their children unconditionally. However, children often perceive that they are loved conditionally. For example, when bringing a paper home from school, a child might think, "This is the best job I've ever done on a paper. I'll bet my parents will be very proud of me." All would be well if the parents said, "Honey, this is the best job you've ever done on a paper. We're really satisfied with the effort you've put into it." But the parents might believe that "I should always point out ways my child can improve, because that's what love is all about—making sure our loved ones do their best." In such a case, they might spend ten or twenty minutes going over the paper and picking out areas that could be improved. The child would then walk away feeling depressed and thinking, "Even when I've done my best, it's never good enough for my parents," perceiving the parents' act of love as a demonstration of rejection.

Such a misunderstanding can have crucial consequences, since the children's perceptions of the degree of closeness and trust they have with their parents and teachers can influence the very course of their lives. When young people lack close and trusting relationships with significant adults, they usually turn to their peers.

Research from the Search Institute has shown that peer influence correlates closely with the rise in rebellion, resistance, chemical abuse, and promiscuity. Children who have strong perceptions of closeness and trust with significant adults are highly resistant to peer influence and are more heavily influenced by those adults who validate them for who they are.

The Search Institute conducted an extensive study in which they asked young people this question: "If you had a serious problem in your life, who would you prefer to discuss it with to get help and gain insight?" The results indicated overwhelmingly that young people would prefer to talk to their parents in such circumstances. However, when asked who they felt they could actually approach to be listened to and taken seriously, the majority responded this way: "No matter how much I wish I could go to my parents, I could not. They already act toward me as if I were stupid and inadequate, and they seem to feel as if I'm always letting them down. My friends are the only ones who will listen to me and take me seriously, so I talk with them even though I know they don't know any more about life than I do."

EXPECTATIONS AND PERCEPTIONS

DURING THE EARLY 1970S, Dr. Fred Streit conducted a study in eastern Pennsylvania in which 6,000 adolescents between twelve and eighteen were anonymously asked a great many questions. Along with requests for information about school attitudes, drug use and abuse, sexuality, church attendance, alienation, and peer influence, they were asked to describe their family, with the following answer choices:

- We are very close.
- We are somewhat close.
- We are not too close.
- We are not close at all.

The analysis showed that children who believed that their family was not close at all reported that they:

- weren't happy most of the time,
- felt life was boring,
- liked to do things to shock people,
- felt they have less fun than most people,
- seldom felt close to people,
- didn't care about their grades in school,
- were not concerned about getting along with their parents,
- were not concerned about living up to their religious and moral training,
- felt that they were not getting a good education, and
- didn't expect to go to college.

Clear communication, caring, helping, love, sharing, touching, giving, nurturing—all these and more of the good things in life are considered to be elements of a close family.

These youths also said that they went along with the peer group to use drugs, drink alcohol, and commit crimes.

For about a year, the researchers tried to define "a close family." Clear communication, caring, helping, love, sharing, touching, giving, nurturing—all these and more of the good things in life are considered to be elements of a close family. But in seeking an answer to what is a close family, it became clear that the closeness of a family was not something that could be directly measured by someone outside that family. It really didn't matter what any outside observer thought about family relationships or closeness. What did matter was what the youngster believed about the closeness of his or her family. The child behaved in a way consistent with what he or she perceived in the family.

Dr. Streit found that twenty-six factors were involved with how a child believed his or her parents were acting. These factors were described using eight clusters. The eight clusters and the factors within them are as follows:

1. *Love:* Positive evaluation, sharing, expressing affection, emotional support
2. *Loving control:* Intellectual stimulation, child centeredness, possessiveness, protectiveness

3. *Control:* Intrusiveness, suppression of aggression, control through guilt, parental direction

4. *Hostile control:* Strictness, punishment, nagging

5. *Hostility:* Irritability, negative evaluation, rejection

6. *Hostile freedom:* Neglect, ignoring

7. *Freedom:* Extreme freedom, lax discipline

8. *Loving freedom:* Moderate freedom, encouraging sociability, encouraging independent thinking, egalitarian treatment

Then, the pieces of the puzzle came together. It was possible to measure how children saw their parents behaving toward them. This measurement is unique to each child and had to be related only to his or her behavior if it was to have any meaning.

Streit and his colleagues did a new series of studies that asked about each of the dimensions and, at the same time, drug and alcohol use. The results were clear and intriguing in that it was possible to explain the use and abuse of the different drugs by looking at how the adolescent perceived the way his or her parents were acting.

Then, in what is known as a double blind study (in which the participants don't know they are being studied or tested), patients in drug and alcohol rehabilitation centers completed the inventories of their perceptions of their parents. The researchers compared the predictions of drug use made by the equations to what was actually known about the patients' use of drugs. The results were as follows:

> When young people perceive their parents' control over them as loving, designed to move toward autonomy, and when they believe overall that love, care, and respect dominate, they perceive the relationship with their parents as low risk, stable, and low in stress.

Marijuana: 68 percent accuracy

Strong hallucinogens such as LSD, mescaline, peyote: 90 percent accuracy

Sedatives, stimulants, and alcohol: 95 percent accuracy

Narcotics: 100 percent accuracy

Subsequent studies by Streit and others were able to relate perceptions children have of their parents to:

- alcohol use
- types of crime committed
- membership in religious cults
- unwanted adolescent pregnancy
- academic achievement

Strictness Versus Permissiveness

The work of Dr. Streit emphasizes variables relating to control issues in parenting: strictness and permissiveness. The results are shown in the pie diagram in Figure 11.1. Permissiveness, at the top of the pie, is defined as excessive autonomy: too little structure and predictability in the parent-child relationship. Parents using this control style easily give in when children manipulate them.

Excessive control, or strictness—defined earlier as the imposing of excessive power and authority on the child—usually produces rebellion, resistance, hostility, and aggressiveness in children, qualities that leave them at high risk for involvement in one or more of the problem areas.

Love Versus Hostility

The work also emphasizes two other variables relating to parents' love and hostility for their children. In Figure 11.1, love, defined as caring, interest, and respect, is plotted on the right side of the diagram. Hostility, on the left side of the diagram, is defined as neglect, lack of caring, lack of interest, and disrespect.

Four poles, then, appear on the diagram. The researchers polarized love against hostility and permissiveness against strictness. Loving control falls halfway between love and strictness. Toward the top right of the pie is a bias in favor of excessive autonomy. Loving autonomy falls halfway between love and permissiveness. Toward the bottom right of the pie is a bias in favor of excessive control. Moving toward the left from the bottom of the pie, we find a bias in favor of strictness, but this time mixed with hostility. And toward the top left is a bias toward permissiveness mixed with hostility. On the left side we find the range between hostile autonomy and hostile control.

The middle right of the pie (a balance between loving control and loving autonomy) represents the low-risk area of relationships. When young people perceive their parents' control over them as loving, designed to move toward

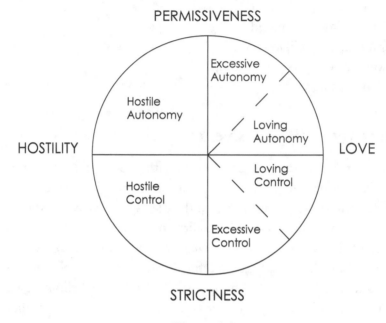

Figure 11.1

autonomy, and when they believe overall that love, care, and respect dominate, they perceive the relationship with their parents as low risk, stable, and low in stress.

> Children who experience parenting that gradually shifts from loving control to loving autonomy in accordance with their developmental readiness are most likely to perceive closeness and trust in their relationships with their parents.

Figure 11.2 illustrates the common drug of choice as correlated with particular parenting styles as perceived by the children involved. Negative behaviors such as manipulation, disrespect, poor attitudes toward life and learning, promiscuity, excessive peer influence, marijuana smoking, and hallucinogen abuse cluster in the area of loving autonomy. When parents err predominately in favor of permissiveness, they can expect those behaviors in relative degrees, depending on the actual degree of their permissiveness.

Behaviors such as rebellion, resistance, hostility, aggressiveness, frequent vandalism, sexual acting out, and alcohol, cocaine, and sedative abuse fall

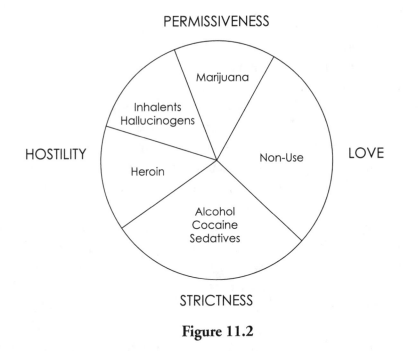

Figure 11.2

into the strictness quadrant of the pie. Hostile control (any control that is neither loving nor respectful) is a very expensive strategy for both children and adults. Parents who adopt a strict and hostile style can expect these behaviors in their children.

Moving from Loving Control to Loving Autonomy

Dr. Streit's work on perceptions and expectations confirms that young children need loving control. As children mature and become ready and able to handle more responsibility, they respond to increasing loving autonomy. Children who experience parenting that gradually shifts from loving control to loving autonomy in accordance with their developmental readiness are most likely to perceive closeness and trust in their relationships with their parents. Such children achieve high levels of productivity, achievement, and resistance to negative peer influence.

The following vignettes dramatize four parenting styles. Each parent is responding to a teenager's request to spend the weekend with a friend.

1. *Hostile autonomy:* "Hey, whatever. We'll see you around." The parent allows the teenager to do whatever she desires but shows a lack of interest, involvement, and care.

2. *Loving autonomy:* "Son, I know you have to put together your schedule for the weekend, but I would appreciate it if you would let me know what you decide." This teenager also gets to do what he wants but lacks guidelines and is required to take no responsibility.

3. *Hostile control:* "You know better than that. You're grounded for a month. Maybe two months. You may never go out again as long as you live." This teenager is on restriction but is filled with hostility because love and respect are lacking.

4. *Loving control:* "Sounds like fun to me. Let me know your plans and what you think is a reasonable time for you to come home. Then I'll give you my ideas on what is reasonable. When we're in agreement, we'll go over the consequences of what will happen if you're late. I'll call your friend's parents to make sure an adult will be available at all times."

Many parents react with skepticism when we endorse the last response here of loving control. They simply do not believe it will work with teenagers. They tell us they are used to giving in to their teenagers' manipulations or revert to using hostile control. Teenagers may not respond at first to a firm but loving approach when they are used to other extremes, but eventually they will. The parents' confidence in the approach is a key to its success. Also important are sincere, loving concern, a tone of voice that conveys respect for the child's dignity, and unwavering patience.

> The parents' confidence in the loving control approach is a key to its success.

The parenting model presented in this book allows us to control the variables of strictness versus permissiveness and love versus hostility. Our methods allow parents and teachers to exercise control firmly but with respect, so that young people will perceive their control as supportive, not as a barrier or an act of aggression. The development of the skills and perceptions of capability they foster in children allows parents and teachers to move toward loving autonomy in their approach to children, who, as a result, develop maturity and a deeply ingrained sense of responsibility.

IT'S NEVER TOO LATE

WE'VE HEARD MANY PARENTS CRY, "Good grief! I've already made so many mistakes. Is it too late?"

It is never too late. Any improvement in parents' and teachers' approach will yield improved results. Dr. Streit's subsequent work with interventions that change adult behavior shows that the subsequent effects were positive in 85 percent of the cases.

Jane's tendency was to err in the direction of permissiveness, because she was staunchly opposed to the humiliation children often experience as a result of strictness. During the writing of this book, she learned that her son was using marijuana. In her zeal to correct the situation, she actually overcorrected, becoming excessively strict. He accelerated his rebellious behavior, even deciding to try a hallucinogenic drug. He had heard from friends that if he took eight motion sickness pills, he would experience a "real trip."

On a camping trip with family and friends, the boy and his friend Jimmy pitched a tent on an island in a lake about two hundred yards from shore and the family camper. The first night was uneventful. The adults checked on the boys several times during the day to see whether they needed anything or wanted to come to shore. They declined, indicating that they were having a good time practicing survival skills.

On the second night, each took eight motion sickness pills and, indeed, they both started hallucinating. Owing to the effects of the drug, it was difficult to obtain a clear story of what had happened during the night, but apparently they didn't enjoy the experience as much as they thought they would and decided to try to sleep it off.

In the wee hours of the morning both boys woke up, still hallucinating. Jimmy tried to swim for shore. But he didn't make it. Jimmy drowned.

This was a terrible lesson to learn and an awful price to pay for the knowledge gained. Jimmy's own parents felt strongly that Jimmy's death was a message that could save others. In tune with their spiritual response, Jane wrote the following poem for Jimmy:

> Jimmy is dead.
> His friends and loved ones grieve.

He was such a joy!
We were not ready for him to leave.

But Jimmy gave his life
That perhaps one more might live.
His mission even greater
If tens or hundreds learn and live.

It was only a motion sickness pill.
But "friends" said, "Take eight
If you want a real thrill—
A 'trip' that is really great."

These "friends" were too blind to see
The dangers of this "high."
"Don't think of consequences.
Have fun now, and fly."

"What do parents know?
They just want to spoil our fun.
They talk about the future.
Who cares! Now is our time in the sun!"

And so, Jimmy is dead.
But he speaks from the grave:
"My death will not be in vain
If even one of you it saves.

"Please tell all your friends
So even more might hear.
Kids are not as smart as they think
When they ignore what their parents fear.

"Tell everyone you see.
Let all your friends know.
Parents hassle you about drugs
Because they love you so.

"My mission on earth is over.
But please join now with me.
Let my death give meaning to your message.
Together we can help others be free.

"Free to think for themselves.
Free to listen to those who know.
Free to have courage—
And know when it is smart to say, 'No!'

"Do not grieve for me.
I am in a wonderful place above.
But do not forget my message:
'Get high on life and love!'"

It's easy to say that mistakes are opportunities for learning, but it's sometimes difficult to believe this when we are experiencing the consequences. It takes true understanding and insight to focus on solutions rather than on blame.

After Jimmy's death, Jane called Steve, three thousand miles away, to tell him what had happened. She said, "If you want me to withdraw from this book project, I will. I can understand that you might not want my name associated with what you're doing."

Very perceptively, Steve replied, "I want you to participate now more than ever. What you learn from this and share with others will be very helpful to many." He suggested that Jane eliminate the barriers and engage in active listening. These two very simple activities—simple because they both involve doing nothing but remaining open and sensitive to what is already there—resulted in a transformation of the relationship between Jane and her son.

By increasing her efforts to eliminate the barriers and quietly listening to her son, Jane created an environment of support. Her son opened up and talked more than she thought he could. When he felt that she was listening and taking him seriously, he became willing to listen, too—especially since Jane's messages contained none of the barriers identified in the book. The closeness and trust mother and son developed as a result of this experience resulted in some dramatic improvements in their lives. In their family meetings they have discussed the importance of the children's contributions to the family, and during these meetings the family carefully structures responsibilities for every privilege. Jane learned the importance of taking the time simply to relax in the same room with her children, to be available to answer their questions, and to enjoy the children as individuals. These principles do work to develop capable young people no matter when we start.

> Once people believe they are capable, significant, and potentially influential (the first three perceptions of the Significant Seven), the Alcoholics Anonymous program helps them practice the rest of the Significant Seven skills.

This does not mean we have to be perfect and use effective parenting principles all the time. Such a practice would be nice, but it is not realistic. Fortunately, these parenting principles can help us correct the problems we create when we don't use them. We were fascinated to hear that airline pilots are at least slightly off course 90 percent of the time. The crew simply uses navigation skills to get the plane back on course.

Parents are also off the course of effective parenting much of the time. While off course, we often help create some interesting problems and dilemmas. Fortunately, we can use the skills outlined in this book to find solutions. We then model for our children that mistakes are wonderful opportunities to learn—and that often we have more opportunities to create closeness and trust while fixing mistakes than we would have had without the mistakes.

ALCOHOLICS ANONYMOUS: DEVELOPING CAPABLE PEOPLE

PERHAPS OUR DEEPEST INSIGHT INTO the process of developing capable people comes from an analysis of the changes that take place in people who successfully go through the Alcoholics Anonymous recovery program. When we compare the millions of people who, over the last fifty years, have transformed themselves from dependent, vulnerable, inadequate people into capable, growing, stable people with those who have gone through the program but without making changes, we see the following results in the first group.

The first step to recovery is a perceptual change—from "I am the way I am" to "I am capable of learning to be different and of taking initiative in my life."

The second step is another perceptual change—from "My life is meaningless, and I don't matter to anyone anyway" to "There is a power greater than myself that gives life meaning and purpose, and I have significance when I contribute to the recovery process of others."

The third step is acquiring the perception that "although I am powerless over chemicals, I am not powerless over the choices that bring them into my life. Until I accept responsibility for my choices, I will always be a victim. I can be a victor when I accept the fact that I cannot control all circumstances of my life but that I can control what I do about those circumstances and what I allow myself to feel about them."

Once people believe they are capable, significant, and potentially influential (the first three perceptions of the Significant Seven), the Alcoholics Anonymous program helps them practice the rest of the Significant Seven skills.

When we identify the changes in perceptions and skills that occur in these successful people, we have a basic understanding of the core of the habilitation process. This insight then serves as a basis for effective prevention, intervention, and treatment programs. Dr. Bob and Bill W. (they chose to withhold their last names to remain anonymous) foresaw the potential convergence of prevention, intervention, and treatment more than fifty years ago, when they wrote in the first edition of *The Blue Book of Alcoholics Anonymous* that "these are essential principles that we must share with our entire culture, and especially the alcoholic." Later, they became concerned that their zeal to save the culture would overshadow their concern for the alcoholic, so they deleted all references to sharing with the entire culture in subsequent editions of *The Blue Book*. But their original insight has been borne out: principles that have been successful in enabling alcoholics to recover have great relevance to other troubled groups in our culture.

DON'T OVERLOOK THE INFLUENCE OF DRUGS

IT IS A TRAGIC FACT of life in the United States that Americans are the world's greatest consumers of illicit drugs. The general availability and widespread use of these substances make them a major barrier to the realizing of potential in both children and adults. All the strategies in this book for raising successful children are proven contributors to drug abuse prevention, intervention, and treatment. However, there is no substitute for an informed, aware parent who actively develops a child's understanding of how and when to confront peer pressure as it applies to chemical use.

Alcoholism and other patterns of chemical dependency show a strong hereditary component. This fact alone makes it important that we all learn our family histories and share them with our children. For many individuals, the only responsible use of drugs and alcohol is no use at all. Furthermore, for people through age twenty the only responsible use of alcohol and psychoactive drugs, such as hallucinogens, marijuana, and cocaine, is that conducted under medical supervision. Human development is highly sensitive to chemicals during the growth and pubescent years.

Although our knowledge of these issues is continually expanding, patterns of drug use change consistently as fads and new chemicals emerge. For this reason, most books and pamphlets are dated before they are even published. Parents and other concerned individuals are well advised to form a relationship with local, state, and national groups seeking to keep the public informed. The following general list should provide sufficient information in the form of newsletters and printed data for local groups in any area of the country:

1. The White House Office for Drug Abuse Policy
2. The National Institute on Drug Abuse (NIDA)
3. The National Institute on Alcoholism (NIAAA)
4. The National Federation of Parents for Drug Free Youth (NFP)
5. Parent Resources in Drug Education (PRIDE, call 1-800-241-7946 twenty-four hours a day for information)

In addition, every state has designated drug and alcohol abuse prevention coordinators. Contact them through the NIDA or your state government.

People often ask us, "How soon should we start to become active in dealing with drug abuse?" We believe that the issue should be discussed in the family from the time the children are very young, since children are exposed to drug taking and drinking through television and other media. Too many parents have waited until their children have reached adolescence only to discover that the exposure had begun long ago and the best time for prevention had passed before they were aware of the need. Basically, if you care, be aware! It is our hope that you will recognize that to emerge successfully from adolescence free of substance abuse, children and parents must practice the Significant Seven principles in their relationships.

12

The Price of Change

WHAT PRICE ARE we willing to pay to ensure that our young people are prepared to be mature adults? Will Rogers taught it this way: "Quality is a lot like buying oats. If you want fresh, clean, first-quality oats, you have to pay a fair price. But if you can be satisfied with oats that have been through the horse, they come a lot cheaper."

The social changes outlined at the beginning of this book are permanent. There is no doubt that these changes have created the problems we have identified. But they have also created unlimited opportunities. Given our confidence in our strategies for solving the problems, we can also assert that there has never been a better time for children to realize their full potential for success.

The price adults must pay for this rich opportunity is the transformation of their approach to child rearing in both the home and the classroom. We see a great and increasing willingness to pay this price among the parents and teachers with whom we interact. Each year we travel throughout the United States and to other countries. Everywhere, we have witnessed a shift toward greater openness. Parents and educators want to know how to be more productively involved with young people. More parents and educators than ever are willing to make the efforts necessary once they know what to do.

At first, new methods and skills can seem awkward. You should expect that and not become unnerved. The key to feeling comfortable with these concepts is to accept the initial awkwardness as natural. In addition, here are some other steps you can take to feel at home with these concepts:

1. Change your own perceptions of how to attain closeness and trust with your children and/or students. It is necessary to change attitudes that promote demands and threats into those that promote warmth, interest, and invitation.

2. Practice slowly. You might start with the simple trick of becoming a closet listener. Practice listening without even letting anyone know what you are doing. Remember, part of being a closet listener is eliminating the five barriers discussed in chapter 4. It is impossible to listen when these barriers are still in place. Allow yourself to become aware of how much you can accomplish by apparently doing nothing. Nothing can become a very important something when you spend time actively listening to children.

3. Practice understanding the perceptions of young people. This will grow easier as you become truly interested, and your interest will grow when you sincerely listen to their point of view. Once you have mastered closet listening, practice understanding children's perceptions through the EIAG process: "Let me be sure I understand. How do you see the situation? What things do you see happening for you? Why is that important to you? How will that have an impact on you?"

Within the atmosphere of closeness and trust created by these steps, young people will grow increasingly interested in your perceptions. And you can further enhance their interest by using the formula "I feel . . . about . . . because . . ."

PERFECTION IS NOT A REQUIREMENT

WE ARE NOT SUGGESTING PERFECTION as a goal. Children are resilient and forgiving, and one or two adultisms slipping into an otherwise respectful atmosphere won't be the end of the world. The idea is to keep improving as we work to encourage and motivate our young people toward their own improvement. The following story illustrates how relatively unimportant a little backsliding can be when the effort toward improvement is consistently practiced.

One day, shortly after writing an early draft of this book, Steve was driving home and saw his oldest daughter riding one of the family's horses and tugging on its mouth. Furious, he locked all four wheels, slid to a stop, leaped a five-foot fence, pulled the girl down off the horse, and said, "That's it! You will never ride a horse again as long as you live! That I should live to see the day that a child of mine would do such a thing to an animal! Don't even touch that horse! I will walk it to the barn myself!"

What an explosion! It felt great.

About an hour later the girl came in to talk with her father. "Dad, have you calmed down enough yet to talk?"

Steve rubbed it in. "I really never expected to see anything like that. I was really absolutely furious."

"You had every right to be angry," she said. "I shouldn't have been riding the horse when I was in a foul mood."

"Then what is there to discuss?" asked Steve.

"I just wanted to make sure you meant it when you said I could never ride a horse again as long as I lived, because you've signed me up for the Nationals and I wondered if I should make other plans for the summer."

"I guess I was a bit heavy-handed," Steve admitted.

"I thought so, too," said the girl.

"But what were you expecting?" Steve asked.

"Well, when you were in a more rational frame of mind, we agreed that if we kids abused the horse, we would have to give up the privilege of riding it for thirty days or, if it was real serious, for six weeks."

"What do you think is called for?" he asked.

"Thirty days."

"I was thinking of six weeks."

"Could we make it five?"

In this example, we see a young person who had not experienced her father's projected anger for a long time. She also understood that the worst time to deal with people's feelings is when they are in the middle of them. Her way of handling the situation was directly related to her perceptions, skills, and capabilities. She was motivated by her belief that if she exercised some self-discipline and judgment and chose her time well, she could influence what happened to her.

MOTIVATION AND SELF-ENCOURAGEMENT

CHANGING OUR WAYS OF INTERRELATING with our children takes strong motivation. Our motivation depends on our overall perceptions of ourselves

> We grow and change much faster when we shed discouraging thoughts about what we have failed to accomplish.

and our capabilities, and these are reflected in those ideas that dominate our thinking. When we want to move across a new frontier, we must imagine ourselves as we wish to be and focus on the specific changes we need to make.

Spending a few moments a day in guided meditation and imagery is an excellent technique for ensuring that you maintain your enthusiasm for trying the new skills you just learned. The following is a prepared guided meditation. Use it by first reading it into a tape recorder. Next, make yourself comfortable, listen to it, and follow the suggestions contained in it.

Think back over the chapters you have read and ask yourself:

1. "What is the most important thing I have gotten in touch with or come to realize, or what behavior change do I want to make as a result of reading this book?"

2. Focus on the thought, realization, motivation, or behavior change you would like to make. Reflect for a moment as to why it impresses you as important right now. How can it make a difference in your life and/or your children's lives? Why did it strike you as important?

3. Leave that reflection and imagine yourself actively seeking the opportunity to do something with your new awareness or knowledge. Where is the first place you intend to apply it? Envision a situation. Imagine yourself thinking, doing, and feeling exactly as you wish in that situation.

4. In your heart, complete the following statement: "As a result of this awareness, the first thing I will do at the first opportunity is . . ."

5. Before you go to bed at night, take a leisure moment and re-create that thought process for yourself. Turn that thought over to your superconsciousness—the thoughts and ideas that fill your mind when you are not thinking of anything in particular—and then go to sleep.

If you follow this guided meditation for three days or more, you will begin to move spontaneously in the desired direction. Each time, reinforce any significant learning with a clear image of what you can do with it, and the image will help you learn, grow, and change.

We grow and change much faster when we shed discouraging thoughts about what we have failed to accomplish. When we re-create our perceived failures, our superconsciousness chatters away throughout the night, sending us messages of inadequacy that burn out our motivation, lock us into a negative frame of mind, and destroy our sleep. If it is important that we help young people focus their superconsciousness on possibilities, then it is clear that we must discipline ourselves in that same process. Negative thinking is self-defeating. It focuses on "What if? If only . . . I should have. Why didn't I?"

To buoy ourselves into a positive attitude, no matter what we accomplished during the day, our last conscious thought before going to sleep should be either an inventory of our contributions or a clear vision of what we will contribute tomorrow as a result of the learning of the day.

TAKING THE FIRST STEP

A FATHER WHO PARTICIPATED IN one of our three-day intensive training programs tried this meditation process on the way home. He realized that he was investing too little time in his relationship with his young son and decided to work conscientiously to upgrade it. In the guided imagery, he envisioned himself as being responsive to his son on a regular basis.

When he announced his intentions to his wife, she quipped, "Well, that ought to last at least two days"—not a very encouraging response.

He replied, "This time I think I have a handle on it."

Over the next week this father was highly responsive to his son. His dream was coming true. One day he was reading the evening paper when suddenly he became aware that his son had been excitedly trying to communicate something to him, and he had given him only half an ear. The son wandered off, and the father only became aware of what had happened as the door closed. "This is not consistent with my dream," he thought.

Off he went to find the boy, who was sitting with his chin on his hands and staring down the street at some boys playing ball with their dads.

"What was it you wanted, Son?" asked the father.

"Oh, nothing," said the boy.

The father persisted, "Now, honey, I sensed your excitement. I just realized I wasn't paying attention to what you were saying. I really want to know."

"OK, Dad. I'm not big enough to play ball very well, but the other boys down the street are going hiking with their dads. I think I could do that if you'd be willing to go with me."

The father said, "Sure, Son. I'd like that a lot. Let's take a trip together. I'll organize it."

Then a little bell went off in his head. In the workshop he had learned that when you treat children as objects or recipients of your actions, you invalidate them. He remembered that he should be making his son an asset in his own efforts in order to affirm him. So he said, "Son, let's work together on this. Why don't you talk with your friends and find out some good places to go. Get back to me on it, and we'll plan the trip together."

The boy immediately went off to get the information from his friends. Later, father and son decided on a destination. The father avoided the temptation to be directing and said, "Now help me think of the things we need to take for the trip."

The little boy said, "We need something to eat and drink and a few other odds and ends."

They made a list and divided up the responsibilities. They even got some canvas, did some stitching, and made a little knapsack instead of buying one.

On the evening before they planned to leave, the father was delayed a little at work. When he came home, he found his son asleep on his knapsack by the door—a precaution against his father leaving him behind. The dad tucked the boy into bed and early in the morning carried him out to the car still asleep and drove off. Just as the dawn was appearing, the little boy woke up, looked around, and smiled. He was thrilled at the sight of the mountains. The father stopped the car, and the two stepped out of the car to look at a small peak jutting from the valley. The son said, "Gee, that's really fantastic. We're going to see what the world looks like up there!"

They set off up the trail and began discovering the joy of being together in the outdoors—watching little minnows in the stream and wading in with bare feet. It was early afternoon before they reached the peak.

"What did you bring to eat?" the father asked.

"Cookies and lemonade," answered the boy.

He had filled the whole pack with cookies and lemonade. They ate and drank while they enjoyed the beauty of the fading afternoon. They forgot to watch the time, and suddenly they realized that it was going to be a race to make it back to the car before dark. They took what they thought would be a shortcut. It was almost dark when they came upon a little tumble-down trapper's cabin. There was a woodpile at the side of the cabin, so they decided not to take a chance on getting lost in the woods. They had enough lemonade and cookies left to make it through the night.

In many ways, this story captures the essence of this book. The father was willing to do many things that embody effective parenting.

They brought in some firewood and started a little fire in the fireplace. Then they sat together watching the fire and eating cookies and lemonade. When the fire started to burn down, the father asked the little boy to go out to the woodpile for more.

"Sure, Dad," the boy answered happily.

He jumped up and went around a little corner of the cabin. The father sat there looking into the fire until it had almost burned down, and his son still hadn't come back. He got a little nervous and went to find his son. He went around the little corner in the cabin, and there was the little boy standing at the door looking out.

"What's the matter, Son?" asked the father.

"It's dark out there, Dad. I can't see the woodpile."

"So how far can you see?"

"Just about one step outside the door, Dad."

"Well, take it, Son."

The little boy took one step, and his father asked, "Now how far can you see?"

"Just about one more step, Dad."

His father said, "Go ahead and take it."

And step by step the boy made his way to the woodpile. When he turned around, the light in the doorway guided him back.

In many ways, this story captures the essence of this book. The father was willing to do many things that embody effective parenting:

1. He was willing to learn more about effective parenting.

2. He was willing to change his behavior in accordance with his new awareness.

3. He saw the value of spending more quality time with his son.

THE THREE R'S OF RECOVERY

1. Recognize (realize mistake)
2. Reconcile (apologize)
3. Resolve (work together on solutions)

4. He learned from his mistakes and started again.
5. He engaged in dialogue.
6. He treated his son as an active participant rather than a passive object.
7. He allowed his son to experience the consequences of his choices.
8. He shared responsibilities with his son.
9. He took time to enjoy life with his son.
10. He allowed his son to take meaningful roles.

This is a good analogy for all of us. The woodpile of our dreams may be a long way off, and it can seem dark out there. Most of us will never see the woodpile when it is time to take the first step. All we will ever get on this planet is one step at a time. All we'll ever be allowed to see is that first step, and it will be different for each of us because our eyes are all at different heights above the ground. The amount of confidence differs. Our legs are of different lengths. No one can take anyone else's first step.

This book has presented a world of possibilities, and many of them may seem far away in the dark. Choose just one thing you would like to work on. Make it something that seems simple to you, perhaps eliminating a single barrier. Take that first step, and you will see the next emerging from the dark. Many people spend their whole life standing in the doorway saying, "I'm not going to take any steps until I see the woodpile." And they stand in the doorway forever.

If, in your effort to take your first step, you get lost for a little while, read some more, join a study group, or call a friend for support until you get a perspective on where that woodpile might be so you can begin to move toward your goal again—one step at a time.

INOCULATION

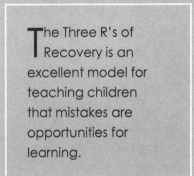

The Three R's of Recovery is an excellent model for teaching children that mistakes are opportunities for learning.

TOGETHER, THE STRATEGIES PRESENTED IN this book help "inoculate" our children against developing the characteristics of high-risk individuals. Most of these activities promote firmness with dignity and respect and teach us to avoid strictness and permissiveness. The following story and suggestions are offered as guidelines to making the essential changes necessary in ourselves.

In Jane's book, *Positive Discipline,* she stresses the importance of using firmness with dignity and respect when interacting with children. Although the philosophy of positive discipline is never humiliating to children, parents sometimes behave in humiliating ways, as this story illustrates:

Recently, in anger, Jane called her eleven-year-old daughter Mary a spoiled brat.

Mary retorted, "Well, don't tell me later that you are sorry."

Jane promised, "You don't have to worry, because I'm not."

Mary went to her bedroom, grabbed her copy of *Positive Discipline,* and wrote "phony" on several pages. Five minutes later she ran to Jane, threw her arms around her mother, and said, "I'm sorry."

Jane said, "I'm sorry, too, honey. I really lost it, didn't I? It is obvious that I was being a spoiled brat when I called you a spoiled brat. I was upset at you for not controlling your behavior, but I didn't control my own behavior. I apologize."

Mary said, "That's OK, Mom, I really was being a brat, and I apologize."

The two then talked about a plan for how they would handle such behavior in the future. Mary was quick to apologize because she has experienced many apologies through a process called the "Three R's of Recovery" (see the sidebar).

Children respond very favorably to this process. Even when they are feeling very angry and resentful toward an adult who has been disrespectful and humiliating, they are quick to forgive when an apology is offered. An apology usually creates an atmosphere of support so that positive work on solutions can take place.

The Three R's of Recovery is an excellent model for teaching children that mistakes are opportunities for learning. Many parents have found that using this process after making a mistake improves the relationship so much that they are actually glad they made the mistake.

> Apologies are only effective when we genuinely recognize that we have behaved in an ineffective manner and want to take steps toward correction.

Parents often ask, "Doesn't an apology undermine your authority with children?"

We reply, "We hope so. We are more interested in cooperation, negotiation, and teaching self-discipline than in maintaining authority."

Too many people consider apologies to be wishy-washy. And they can be when a person is being self-effacing and is apologizing just to please the other person. Apologies are only effective when we genuinely recognize that we have behaved in an ineffective manner and want to take steps toward correction.

A few days after the exchange Jane had with Mary, Mary was talking on the phone with her friend. "Oh, Nancy, you are so stupid," she said. She quickly recovered, saying, "I'm sorry, Nancy. If I call you stupid it means I am being stupid." Mary had learned to be responsible for her own perceptions and to apologize for being disrespectful.

In an earlier chapter, we stated that we should never apologize for our feelings, such as anger, but only for what we might do with our anger that might be disrespectful to another person. The same holds true when we are doing the best we can with whatever skills and understanding we have. Apologizing in such a context is completely inappropriate. We give young people a good example when we forgive ourselves for our own mistakes and learn from them rather than becoming depressed or angry when we make them.

It is never helpful to say, "You are a naughty girl," or even "You did a naughty thing." The constructive reaction is "Whoops, that didn't work. What can we do to fix it?" In such a situation, it is better to call attention to our own mistakes or struggles—for example, "I have always struggled with my feelings, and I don't handle that very well. It's cost me a lot at work, and it's cost me a lot in my relationships. Whenever you need to talk about something, I'll try; I'll do my best." This attitude invites children to help the parent work out a problem. Working to help parents in their struggles can be very affirming to children.

CONSISTENCY

PEOPLE OFTEN MAKE A GREAT issue of consistency, saying, "What can I do when the child's mother, father, or teacher does things differently?"

Children are beautifully equipped to handle inconsistencies between people and their environment. They are very good at adapting to different people and, in fact, thrive on social diversity.

PARENTING WITH PERSPECTIVE

HAVING JOSEPH SOLD INTO EGYPT by his brothers could have been a disaster for Jacob of the Bible. It all depends on your perspective. If what Jacob wanted was his neighbors' approval, the experience would only have been negative. Those neighbors were bound to say, "That man was a prophet and still had a kid sold to the Egyptians by the rest of the family."

But if Jacob's long-term goal was to have his children and descendants thrive and survive, then Joseph's being sold into Egypt was a great blessing. While Jacob's disapproving neighbors died in the famine, his own family moved down to Egypt and joined Joseph.

Judging our performance over the short term is a great mistake. Parents often judge themselves—erroneously—this way: "If I were a better parent, I would have better children." Adam and Eve (in Judeo-Christian traditions) started out walking and talking with God and then went out to begin the first family. Without peer influence, television, MTV, or a history of family "dysfunction," they only batted .500 with their first two sons. What one child experienced as a supportive environment, the other experienced as rejection and favoritism and thus rationalized the first recorded homicide in family history. The first recorded parents in this tradition ended up with one child dead and the other a murderer. Their experience suggests that no matter what you do as a parent, in the end your children will express their individuality. Adam and Eve's story also makes it clear that dealing with two children the same way never guarantees those children the same experience. What one son sees as support, for example, the other may see as rejection.

Perspective is the overall lesson we can glean from Adam and Eve's experience with their children. And a little humor doesn't hurt, either. Laughter is a door to self-forgiveness—and a reminder, sometimes badly needed, that, in spite of the struggle, raising children can be a joyful adventure.

APPENDIX:
A SUMMARY OF RELEVANT
RESEARCH AND EXPERIENCE

SINCE THE FIRST EDITION OF *Raising Self-Reliant Children* was published and given its usage as a text in at least two major training programs in Canada and the United States, we have had constant requests for information about research on the Significant Seven and the programs that are based on them (e.g., the Developing Capable People [DCP] and Developing Capable Young People [DCYP] training programs we have subsequently developed; DCYP is a revision of the original DCP program, and the titles will be used somewhat interchangeably here). The following brief summary of some of the most important research and applications of the concepts advocated in this book was assembled by Dr. Bruce Colston. He is a great friend and an untiring advocate for the principles outlined in this book

Background

PERSISTENT PROBLEMS OF DRUG and alcohol abuse, violence, adolescent pregnancy and parenthood, chronic problems in school, and so forth, are major issues confronting every community in the United States. The struggle with these issues became a national preoccupation in the 1960s and has continued to escalate since then. A wide range of programs and strategies has been attempted over the past forty years, with varying degrees of success. Research continues, and some past and present projects offer criteria, guidelines, and direction for prevention programming.

From 1972 to 1976, an exhaustive analysis of hundreds of research projects and reports in the fields of chemical dependency, juvenile justice, education, and physical and mental health was conducted by the National Drug Abuse Center for Training and Resource Development in Washington, D.C. Among the significant findings of this project with respect to drug and alcohol abuse, violence/antisocial behavior, and poor educational performance were the following:

1. *Collaborative/cooperative learning processes* (including class meetings and positive discipline principles) are particularly effective in kindergarten through sixth grade as long-term prevention strategies.

2. *Informed parents and teachers* who take an advocacy position with young people throughout the developmental years are a most effective prevention/intervention resource.

3. *Mentoring* young people can be an effective prevention, intervention, and/or treatment strategy depending on the type and quality of interaction between the mentor and mentee.

4. *Life skills and prosocial skills development* are consistently effective for adolescent prevention/intervention efforts both proactively (as courses) and reactively (as student assistance/alternative education programs).

5. *Resiliency* in people is a critical factor in treatment, prevention, and intervention efforts.

Research has indicated that the relative strength or weakness of seven essential life resources, the Significant Seven, is directly correlated with resiliency, mentor effectiveness, life skills development, and positive behavioral health outcomes and success in recovery. In addition, the relative strength or weakness of these same life resources is inversely correlated with behavioral health risk at a very high level.

Extensive research indicates that the three perceptions and four skills described in this book strongly influence character, resiliency, behavioral health, maturity, and self-sufficiency. In 1977, these Significant Seven were officially adopted as criteria for prevention, intervention, treatment, and research programs by the U.S. Department of Health, Education, and Welfare (now the Department of Health and Human Services) and the National Institute on Drug Abuse (NIDA) (Alcohol, Drug, and Mental Health Administration, 1977). For a list of the Significant Seven please see the following page.

As people acquire strength in each of these seven areas, they become increasingly less at risk to a wide range of problems, including substance abuse, adolescent pregnancy and parenthood, academic dropout rates, underachievement, and gang involvement (Glenn, 1977, 1978).

In the nearly twenty-five years since the NIDA study, research has steadily accumulated validating the essential reliability of this policy recommendation: Search Institute (youth asset development); Hawkins and Catalano (risk and

THE SIGNIFICANT SEVEN

Resources	*Types of Outcomes*
1. <u>PERCEPTIONS</u> OF PERSONAL CAPABILITIES "I am a capable person who can face problems and challenges and gain strength and wisdom through experience."	**Three pillars of healthy self-concept and healthy self-esteem**
2. <u>PERCEPTIONS</u> OF PERSONAL SIGNIFICANCE "Who I am and what I have to offer in life and relationships is of value—my life has meaning and purpose."	
3. <u>PERCEPTIONS</u> OF PERSONAL INFLUENCE "I am accountable for my actions and choices and have the power to influence my life."	
4. INTRAPERSONAL <u>SKILLS</u> Capacities of self-assessment, self-control, and self-discipline in responding to and dealing with feelings.	**Twin pillars of emotional intelligence, self-discipline, and effective relationships**
5. INTERPERSONAL <u>SKILLS</u> Capacities to communicate, cooperate, negotiate, share, empathize, resolve conflicts, and listen effectively when dealing with people.	
6. SYSTEMIC <u>SKILLS</u> Sufficient capacities in responsibility, adaptability, and flexibility to function effectively within life systems, (social, legal, family, school, environment, etc.)	**Social and personal responsibility**
7. JUDGMENT <u>SKILLS</u> Resources and capacities for planning, identifying choices and making decisions based on wisdom and moral and ethical principles such as honesty, respect, fairness, equality, and compassion—developing "mature judgment."	**Decision making, moral and ethical development**

protective factors); Hawkins (Seattle Intervention Project); Bernard (resiliency); PIRE, (social competency and refusal skills); Reasoner (healthy self-esteem); Olson (family cohesiveness]; and Pransky (prevention). *All* of these researchers have specifically identified several or all of the seven elements on which *Raising Self-Reliant Children* and DCP and DCYP are based as major contributors to successful prevention outcomes.

Responding to These Issues

IN 1982, H. STEPHEN GLENN piloted the first version of the Developing Capable People program. In the development of DCP/DCYP programs, formative research drew from many sources. Research on relationships between adults and young people (including Olson's scales of cohesiveness) has consistently identified respect, affirmation, and trust as the most influential factors. One very interesting and useful study was conducted in 1975 by Jim Tunney and James Jenkins, who asked teachers to assess the degree to which they cared for and respected their students (90 percent and 80 percent, respectively, chose 8 or higher on a scale of 10). They then asked their students to indicate the degree to which they believed their teacher cared for and/or respected them (30 percent and 25 percent, respectively, chose 8 or higher on the same 10-point scale).

As part of his work as director of both the Southeast Regional Training Center (1972–75) and the National Drug Abuse Center for Training and Resource Development (1976–77), Glenn conducted informal research as part of a number of training development projects. In one study, he sought to determine why the messages of care and respect (which encourage trust) were not getting through adequately. He identified those behaviors that teachers perceived to be supportive and caring of students and those behaviors that students interpreted as uncaring and/or disrespectful. Among the results were that many of the traditional adult behaviors for dealing with youth were preventing the messages of care and respect from getting through, which helps explain some of the findings of Tunney and Jenkins.

Glenn also asked people to respond to the following questions. "I believe I am 'respected' in a relationship when I experience _____ " and "I believe I am 'not respected' in a relationship when I experience

_____." He also did the same with *cared for, trusted,* and similar terms. He synthesized these findings and developed a relationship inventory as a training activity that was then used to have people assess, on a 7-point scale, the qualities of their relationships with significant adults and their perceptions of care, respect, and trust. Over forty specific adult behaviors were found to be correlated with perceptions of respect, care, and/or supportive of trust, and ten specific behaviors were correlated with perceptions of a lack of care, respect, and/or trust.

After doing similar work with the Significant Seven and finding that most of the variables influencing relationships also affected the development of critical life resources, Glenn created the DCP and DCYP training programs. They have been specifically designed to teach people how they can nurture the development of these resources in others to produce the types of positive outcomes previously discussed. These programs have demonstrated exceptional capacity to do so.

DCP and Family Cohesiveness

RESEARCH OVER THE PAST THIRTY years has demonstrated that family cohesiveness is one of the best and most consistent predictors of delinquency, drug abuse, gang involvement, chronic problems in school, and other behavioral health issues. Among the critical factors that influence cohesiveness are respect, affirmation, and trust, which are extremely important prosocial resources. D. H. Olson's (1985) Scales of Family Cohesiveness is a standardized research tool for measuring this variable and has been a consistently reliable predictor of these phenomena.

These primary factors also directly affect more than ten of the assets identified by Search Institute and support an additional block of ten. Twenty or more assets represent a substantial reduction in the probability of high-risk behavior, according to the Search Institute. Cohesiveness is also significant in influencing risk and protective factors as identified by David Hawkins, Lisher, Catalano, and Howard (1986) in their highly regarded model, especially in the area of family bonding.

Research conducted by William McNabb (1990), based on controlled studies using Olson's scales, demonstrated that DCP constitutes a powerful program for increasing family cohesiveness. Young people who had one or more of their parents involved in the program showed statistically significant increases in their perceptions of family cohesiveness regardless of gender or geography. Children ages five to nine had significantly higher family cohesion scores than older children.

DCP and Mentoring

IN A 1996 STATEWIDE PROJECT, Kirk Astroth, extension 4-H specialist at Montana State University, and Scott Lorbeer conducted a criterion-based assessment of fifteen programs for training adults to work effectively with children and youth. The committee found Developing Capable People to be most responsive to its criteria. Glenn trained an initial cadre of leaders to implement the program statewide. He also developed two trainers who subsequently trained additional leaders.

Researchers from the Montana State University Survey Research Center then conducted an eighteen-month follow-up study of one thousand adults who received DCP training as support for their role as surrogate parents (mentors). The study focused on twenty-nine specific behaviors that the program tried to impact. Of these, twenty-one were positive behaviors, while eight were negative. The Montana research team found that the twenty-one "builder" behaviors and the eight "barrier" behaviors were measurable. They developed and validated a survey instrument for pre- and posttesting and administered it at various points throughout the research period.

The findings showed statistically significant change in all twenty-nine behaviors, which increased over time, indicating that the training process is producing sustained second-order change. An additional noteworthy aspect of the study is the fact that the training was conducted by "first- and second-generation" leaders. This demonstrates that the materials and the leadership development process are capable of disseminating the program effectively through local capacity building.

This study demonstrates that the DCP program is effective in producing significant improvement in all twenty-nine behaviors on an ongoing basis. It also indicates a need for specifically targeted training for adults who seek to mentor young people if we are to maximize the value of such interaction. At the time of this writing, Glenn is doing just that by conducting statewide mentor training for the California Mentor Initiative using the DCYP program.

NPERN and Family Strengths

IN 1982, THE National Prevention and Education Research Network (NPERN) conducted an independent impact study of the initial DCP model on families in South Carolina. It developed and validated a Family Strengths Inventory that measures family cohesiveness, effective discipline processes, family structure, locus of control, bonding, and so forth. The study showed (through a pretest/posttest design with control groups) that DCP had significant measurable positive impact on all of these variables regardless of ethnicity, family income, education levels, and other characteristics (Wagner, 1983).

Orange County Public Schools

IN 1991, WILLIAM R. BROWN of the University of Central Florida and Data Analysts and Research Consultants, Inc., conducted an extensive impact study for the Orange County Public Schools in Orlando, Florida, to determine the effectiveness of its "Comprehensive Drug/Alcohol Abuse Prevention Training Program for School-Site Teachers, Counselors, Administrators, Support Staff, and Parents." The DCP program was the primary strategy the school system selected. The study showed that DCP significantly improved teacher morale and effectiveness, discipline, motivation and achievement for students, and parent effectiveness and support. The study used a set of validated instruments and a pretest/posttest format with control groups. It also showed a direct positive effect on reported incidence of behavioral health-related episodes.

An additional element of this project was that of providing the DCP training for court-mandated parents. The program showed an ability to produce significant changes in attitude and behavior even in parents who were initially hostile and/or resistant. The study also indicated the potential for reducing recidivism within the juvenile justice system. These results have been replicated in several other studies with parents and other inmates along with their significant others in jails and in the probation system including Utah County, Utah, and Snohomish County, Washington. Another study is currently being conducted by Indiana University and the Family Services Association in Bloomington, Indiana.

The NPERN study also evaluated first- and second generation leaders and various elements of the training program for their overall contributions to the outcomes. The conclusions were that the DCP program is relatively easy to implement and quite cost-effective and produces measurable results in reducing negative behaviors in young people and increasing positive outcomes for parents, educators and students.

Parent Training

A STUDY BY JUDITH HARPER at the University of Massachusetts in Amherst measured the effects of DCP training on the self-concept and behavior of mothers. Using an interview instrument with multiple raters, she demonstrated that mothers who participated in the DCP training showed significant increases in healthy self-concept, interpersonal skills, and effectiveness in working with their children and others. The findings indicate that the DCP program can provide resources for improving mothers' effectiveness in interacting with their children and in reducing their personal stresses.

Jack Pransky, in his 1991 book *A Pound of Prevention: The Critical Need for Society,* reports his findings from studies he conducted with 409 parents from forty-five different DCP classes. His results show a 72 percent reduction in the number of times per week the most troubling child behaviors occurred. In addition, 92 percent of the parents stated that their children's behaviors improved as a result of the course. Interestingly, he found that 91 percent of the parents reported that their own behavior in dealing with their children had changed. Pransky concludes that when these results are repeated over time, one can surmise that it had something to do with the content and process of DCP.

DCYP and Resiliency

RESILIENCY HAS BEEN IDENTIFIED as a critical factor in resistance to and recovery from a wide range of diseases and behavioral health problems. Research on resiliency has consistently identified a number of factors that influence a person's ability to thrive in the face of challenges and adversity.

Among them are such external factors as family cohesiveness, community support, and access to mentors and internal factors such as optimism, healthy self-esteem, a sense of meaning and purpose in life, self-discipline, and prosocial bonding (Benard, 1991; Hawkins et al., 1986).

With the possible exception of community support and access to mentors, DCP is specifically designed to impact most internal and external factors associated with resiliency. Impact studies have shown that DCP does in fact increase family cohesiveness, increase healthy self-esteem, promote positive bonding, and help strengthen personal resources in the areas of self-discipline, interpersonal skills, moral and ethical development, and purposeful living. In other words, it provides a powerful integrated process for preparing adults to foster resiliency and self-sufficiency in young people—of any age.

DCP snd Self-Sufficiency

SINCE 1992, Developing Capable People has been a required training program for adult and family service personnel in Oregon. Since 1995, it has been a foundation program for clients of the welfare system in that state and has involved several thousand individuals. In 199697, the program was recognized as the outstanding training program of the state and received "The Investing in People Award" from the governor of Oregon.

A comprehensive five-year study showed that the DCP training program reduced absenteeism, turnover, and domestic stress for the staff, while increasing teamwork and effectiveness on the job. For clients of the social welfare system, it increased capacity for self-sufficiency and reduced domestic stress and conflict significantly. (In the area of welfare reform, Oregon leads the country, with 98.2 percent of its previously dependent welfare population sustaining half-time or better employment, compared to a national average of 30 percent, according to *USA Today*, August 1, 1999).

DCP/DCYP and Protective Factors

IN STUDIES OF RESILIENCY, childhood predictors, and the prevention of adolescent substance abuse Hawkins et al. (1986) identify a number of "protective factors" that have significant predictive value:

- perceptions of personal competency (in play, school, relationships),

- perceptions of personal significance (a stakeholder, contributor in the community, family, school),

- perceptions of oneself as accountable for and able to influence one's life (internal locus of control, sense of empowerment),

- self-discipline,

- interpersonal competency,

- systems skills (responsibility, flexibility, decision-making skills),

- judgment (goal orientation, prosocial values, abstract reasoning),

- healthy expectations (sense of humor, positive outlook), and

- healthy bonding processes ("cohesiveness" in family, school, community, peer group)

Each of these protective factors is an outcome strongly influenced by the DCP/DCYP programs. Of particular importance is the fostering of cohesiveness as a characteristic of family, school, and community from the perspective of young people.

Youth Asset Development and DCYP

SEARCH INSTITUTE HAS BEEN CONDUCTING research on young people for over forty years, producing many useful reports during that time. Its research contributed directly to the design of DCP/DCYP because it was identified as significant in preparing the NIDA document mentioned previously. In Search's early work, four categories of factors surfaced as having significance for behavioral health risk prediction and/or reduction:

1. Strong perceptions of closeness and trust with significant adults
2. Strength of moral positions (by or beyond eleven years of age)
3. Strong perceptions of a meaningful/contributing role in prosocial institutions (i.e., home, school, community, religious organizations, youth programs, etc.)
4. Healthy self-esteem

Each of these areas has been shown to be inversely correlated with negative peer influence and behavioral health problems. They are directly correlated with positive adult influence, prosocial ideation, and wellness.

Search Institute's most recent reports serve as the basis for the Healthy Communities-Healthy Kids initiatives that are being considered nationwide. The initiative is based on several hundred thousand responses on a series of self-reported survey instruments from many years. Search divided its analysis into internal and external categories, each containing twenty "developmental assets" that it finds to be correlated with the self-reported incidence of such behavioral health issues as alcohol, tobacco, and drug abuse; sexual acting out; antisocial behavior, and academic success. (For a list of these assets, please refer to the 40 Developmental Assets chart on the opposite page.)

Search Institute presents an interpretation of its data that suggests that the greater the number of "assets" reported by individuals, the less likely they are to report high-risk behaviors. In other words, youth whose patterns of responses are positive in fewer than ten of the forty areas are *most likely* to report involvement with drugs of abuse, antisocial behavior, sexual activity, and so forth, whereas youth whose patterns of responses are positive in thirty or more of the forty areas are *least likely* (by a wide margin) to report such behaviors.

Three Issues

Since Search Institutes' research has focused on adolescents twelve to eighteen years old, we believe that the following questions should be raised:

1. How much of what Search Institute is measuring reflects the cumulative effects of earlier experiences?
2. To what extent are the assets "adult driven"?
3. What is necessary to impact youth in ways that enhance the "developmental assets"?

Historically, most prevention programs have directly targeted children and *youth* (curricula, special school programs, clubs, intervention programs, student assistance, etc.) rather than the *adults* who influence them. A significant majority of the assets identified by Search are essentially adult driven; in other words, they are directly and indirectly influenced by the type and quality of

40 Developmental Assets

Search Institute has identified the following building blocks of healthy development that help young people grow up healthy, caring, and responsible.

	CATEGORY	ASSET NAME AND DEFINITION
EXTERNAL ASSETS	**Support**	1. **Family support**—Family life provides high levels of love and support. 2. **Positive family communication**—Young person and her or his parent(s) communicate positively, and young person is willing to seek advice and counsel from parent(s). 3. **Other adult relationships**—Young person receives support from three or more nonparent adults. 4. **Caring neighborhood**—Young person experiences caring neighbors. 5. **Caring school climate**—School provides a caring, encouraging environment. 6. **Parent involvement in schooling**—Parent(s) are actively involved in helping young person succeed in school.
	Empowerment	7. **Community values youth**—Young person perceives that adults in the community value youth. 8. **Youth as resources**—Young people are given useful roles in the community. 9. **Service to others**—Young person serves in the community one hour or more per week. 10. **Safety**—Young person feels safe at home, at school, and in the neighborhood.
	Boundaries & Expectations	11. **Family boundaries**—Family has clear rules and consequences and monitors the young person's whereabouts. 12. **School boundaries**—School provides clear rules and consequences. 13. **Neighborhood boundaries**—Neighbors take responsibility for monitoring young people's behavior. 14. **Adult role models**—Parent(s) and other adults model positive, responsible behavior. 15. **Positive peer influence**—Young person's best friends model responsible behavior. 16. **High expectations**—Both parent(s) and teachers encourage the young person to do well.
	Constructive Use of Time	17. **Creative activities**—Young person spends three or more hours per week in lessons or practice in music, theater, or other arts. 18. **Youth programs**—Young person spends three or more hours per week in sports, clubs, or organizations at school and/or in the community. 19. **Religious community**—Young person spends one or more hours per week in activities in a religious institution. 20. **Time at home**—Young person is out with friends "with nothing special to do" two or fewer nights per week.
INTERNAL ASSETS	**Commitment to Learning**	21. **Achievement motivation**—Young person is motivated to do well in school. 22. **School engagement**—Young person is actively engaged in learning. 23. **Homework**—Young person reports doing at least one hour of homework every school day. 24. **Bonding to school**—Young person cares about her or his school. 25. **Reading for pleasure**—Young person reads for pleasure three or more hours per week.
	Positive Values	26. **Caring**—Young person places high value on helping other people. 27. **Equality and social justice**—Young person places high value on promoting equality and reducing hunger and poverty. 28. **Integrity**—Young person acts on convictions and stands up for her or his beliefs. 29. **Honesty**—Young person "tells the truth even when it is not easy." 30. **Responsibility**—Young person accepts and takes personal responsibility. 31. **Restraint**—Young person believes it is important not to be sexually active or to use alcohol or other drugs.
	Social Competencies	32. **Planning and decision making**—Young person knows how to plan ahead and make choices. 33. **Interpersonal competence**—Young person has empathy, sensitivity, and friendship skills. 34. **Cultural competence**—Young person has knowledge of and comfort with people of different cultural/racial/ethnic backgrounds. 35. **Resistance skills**—Young person can resist negative peer pressure and dangerous situations. 36. **Peaceful conflict resolution**—Young person seeks to resolve conflict nonviolently.
	Positive Identity	37. **Personal power**—Young person feels he or she has control over "things that happen to me." 38. **Self-esteem**—Young person reports having a high self-esteem. 39. **Sense of purpose**—Young person reports that "my life has a purpose." 40. **Positive view of personal future**—Young person is optimistic about her or his personal future.

interaction between young people and parents, teachers, adult mentors, and other adults.

This idea was confirmed by a longitudinal study conducted by Hawkins and others referred to as the Seattle Intervention Project. It is included here as its findings strongly support the process and content of the DCP/DCYP programs with their focus on appropriate adult training and early intervention. More specifically, the Seattle Intervention Project offers evidence that the collaborative learning models, positive discipline principles, class and family meeting models, parent/teacher training processes, and the models of healthy self-esteem and prosocial skills promoted by the DCYP program have long-term positive impact in the areas of violence reduction, alcohol abuse, sexual activity, and pregnancy. A summary of its findings were reported in the *New York Times* (Brody, 1999). For the full study, see the journal *Archives of Pediatrics and Adolescent Medicine,* March 1999.

These findings are further supported by the research of Daniel Goleman (1995) on emotional intelligence that shows significant behavioral health outcomes from the early development of intra- and interpersonal skills—numbers 4 and 5 of the Significant Seven.

There is also evidence that the development of at least thirty assets is easier prior to the onset of puberty than afterward. The greater the level of assets (number and strength) entering adolescence, the more powerful their positive impact is throughout the teenage years. Hawkins et al. (1986), in an extensive review of prevention literature, concluded, "If the goal is to prevent serious maladaptive behavior associated with drug abuse in adolescence, then it may be desirable to focus prevention efforts on those youth who manifest behavior problems, including aggressive and other antisocial behaviors, during the elementary grades" In its original work, Search Institute used the terms "by or beyond the age of eleven" in describing the correlations between the original four categories and behavioral health issues. Asset development prior to the onset of puberty is highly adult driven, as the Seattle Intervention Project demonstrates.

The need to have parents and other adults who work with youth receive appropriate training is also a major point made by the Carnegie Council on Adolescent Development in its report *A Matter of Time: Risk and Opportunity in the Nonschool Hours* (Takanishi and Quinn, 1992). It states, "An immediate first step is for community programs to expand greatly the availability of appropriate training . . . for all adults who work directly with young people." Much research indicates that the greatest value of mentor programs lies in the type and quality of the interaction between the mentor and the mentee (see the "surrogate parenting" study reported by Asroth and Lorbeer, 1996).

Therefore, in any effective youth asset development effort, it is essential to include and emphasize appropriate training, direction, and support for adults, who impact children and youth. *Raising Self-Reliant Children* and the DCYP/DCP training programs are designed to do just that! They prepare adults to positively impact at least thirty-two of the forty assets identified by Search Institute. They directly promote twenty and support twelve of the forty youth assets currently being advocated by Search Institute and the Healthy Communities-Healthy Kids programs.

The Significant Seven and Asset Development

A POWERFUL CORRELATION EXISTS between the Search Institute's twenty "internal assets" and the Significant Seven discussed in this book, demonstrating that as people develop strengths in the Significant Seven, they will attain most, if not all, of the twenty assets. To see this relationship between the internal assets and the Significant Seven more clearly, please refer to Appendix Table 1.

Conclusion

HOW DO *Raising Self-Reliant Children* and the Developing Capable People programs respond to the current emphasis on resiliency and youth asset development in funding criteria for alcohol, tobacco, drug abuse, and violence prevention programs? We hope that this summary has provided the reader with an understanding of how this book and DCP work toward long-term prevention efforts focusing on adult training and youth development.

One of the major reasons we have undertaken putting this research summary together is to demonstrate that the DCP programs and the Significant Seven are:

APPENDIX TABLE 1:
THE RELATIONSHIP BETWEEN THE SIGNIFICANT SEVEN AND THE SEARCH INSTITUTE'S INTERNAL ASSETS

Asset Name	Perceptions of Personal Capability	Perceptions of Personal Significance	Perceptions of Personal Influence	Intrapersonal Skills	Interpersonal Skills	Systemic Skills	Judgment Skills
21. Achievement Motivation			X	X			X
22. School Engagement	X			X			X
23. Homework			X	X			X
24. Bonding to School		X			X		
25. Reading for Pleasure							X
26. Caring		X			X	X	X
27. Equality and Social Justice		X			X	X	X
28. Integrity	X		X	X		X	X

#	Asset							
29.	Honesty	X			X	X		X
30.	Responsibility	X	X		X	X		
31.	Restraint	X	X		X			
32.	Planning and Decision-Making	X	X		X	X		
33.	Interpersonal Competence			X				
34.	Cultural Competence						X	
35.	Resistance Skills	X	X		X	X		
36.	Peaceful Conflict Resolution	X	X	X	X	X		
37.	Personal Power	X	X		X	X		
38.	Self-Esteem	X	X	X	X	X	X	
39.	Sense of Purpose	X					X	
40.	Positive View of Personal Future	X	X	X	X	X	X	X

- based on sound theory in the field;

- effective, as demonstrated through several empirical studies;

- particularly powerful in the areas of adult training and youth development;

- supportive of and supported by other relevant research and theory in the field of prevention and youth development; and, therefore,

- deserving of serious consideration as appropriate long-term prevention programming.

Virtually any program or activity that seeks to promote health, wellness, growth, and/or self-sufficiency in people will find in DCYP/DCP essential foundation elements.

Research Bibliography

ADAMHA. (1977). "State of the Art" In *National Manpower Development and Training Strategy,* 1977.

Astroth, Kirk A., and Scott H. Lorbeer. (1996). *Developing Capable People: A Program with Long Term Benefits.* Research Report, State 4-H Office. Bozeman: Montana State University.

Benard, Bonnie. (1991). *Fostering Resiliency in Kids: Protective Factors in the Family, School, and Community.* Portland, OR: Western Center for Drug-Free Schools.

Brody, Jane E. (1999). "Study Says Social Interaction Averts Risky Teen-Age Behavior." *New York Times,* March 15.

Brown, William R. (1991). *"Developing Capable People": External Evaluator Report.* Orlando, FL: Data Analysts and Research Consultants.

Glenn, H. Stephen. (1997a). "Habilitation as an Alternative to Rehabilitation." *Juvenile Justice Digest* 5, no. 23 (December).

———. (1977b). *Practical Approaches to Strengthening the Family.* Washington, D.C.: American Family Society.

———. (1978). "Toward an Understanding of Prevention." In *Proceedings: 1977 Alcohol and Drug Problems Association National Conference.* Washington, D.C.: Goleman, Daniel. (1995). *Emotional Intelligence.* New York: Bantam.

Harper, Judith C. (1990). "The Effects of the Parenting Course 'Developing Capable People' on the Developmental Stage of Mothers." Ph.D. dissertation, University of Massachusetts, Amherst.

Hawkins, David J., et. al (1986). *Childhood Predictors of Adolescent Substance Abuse: Toward an Empirically Grounded Theory.* Binghamton, NY: Haworth.

McNabb, William H. (1990). *The Developing Capable People Parent Course: A Study of Its Impact on Family Cohesion* Malibu, CA: Graduate School of Education, Pepperdine University.

National Institute on Drug Abuse. (1977). *Manpower and Training Strategy.* Washington, D.C.: Alcohol, Drug Abuse, and Mental Health Administration.

Olson, D. H. (1985). *FACES III.* St. Paul: University of Minnesota, Family Social Science.

Pransky, Jack. (1991). *A Pound of Prevention: The Critical Need for Society.* Burlington, VT: Waterfront.

Takanishi, Ruby, and Jane Quinn, eds. (1992). *A Matter of Time: Risk and Opportunity in the Nonschool Hours.* Washington, D.C.: Carnegie Council on Adolescent Development.

Tunney, James, J., and James Mancel Jenkins. (1975). *A Comparison of Climate as Perceived by Selected Students, Faculty, and Administrators in PASCL, Innovative and Other High Schools.* Los Angeles: University of Southern California.

Wagner, B. (1983). *A Prevention Services Family Demonstration Model.* National Prevention and Research Network.

BIBLIOGRAPHY

Adler, Alfred. *What Life Should Mean to You.* New York: Putnam's, 1958.

Allred, G. Hugh. *How to Strengthen Your Marriage and Family.* Provo, Utah: Brigham Young University Press, 1976.

————. *Mission for Mother: Guiding the Child.* Salt Lake City, Utah: Book Crafts, 1968.

Balswick, J., and C. Macrides. Parental stimulus for adolescent rebellion. *Adolescence,* Vol. X, No. 38 (Summer 1975).

Barnes, G. The development of adolescent drinking behavior: An evaluative review of the impact of the socialization process within the family. *Adolescence,* Vol. XII, No. 48 (1977): 571–591.

Booz-Allen and Hamilton, Inc. An assessment of the needs of and resources for children of alcoholic parents. Prepared for National Institute on Alcohol Abuse and Alcoholism. (Rep. No. PB-241–119; NIAA/NCALI-75/13.) U.S. Nat. Tech. Inform. Serv.; 1974.

Burns, Marilyn. *I Am Not a Short Adult.* Boston and Toronto: Little, Brown, 1977.

Calicchia, J. P. Narcotic addiction and perceived locus of control. *Journal of Clinical Psychology,* Vol. 30 (1973): 499–504.

Canfield, Jack, and Harold Wells. *One Hundred Ways to Enhance Self Concept in the Classroom.* Englewood Cliffs, N.J.: Prentice-Hall, 1976.

Clarke-Stewart, K. Popular primers for parents. *American Psychologist* (April 1978): 359–369.

Cooker, P., and P. Cherchia. Effects of communication skill training on high school students' ability to function as peer group facilitators. *Journal of Counseling Psychology,* Vol. 23, No. 5 (1976): 464–467.

Cork, R. Margaret. *The Forgotten Children.* Ontario, Canada: Alcoholism and Drug Addiction Research Foundation of Ontario, 1969.

Corsini, R. J., and G. Painter. *The Practical Parent.* New York: Harper & Row, 1975.

Dinkmeyer, D., and R. Dreikurs. *Encouraging Children to Learn: The Encouragement Process.* Englewood Cliffs, N.J.: Prentice-Hall, 1963.

———— and Gary D. McKay. *Raising a Responsible Child.* New York: Simon & Schuster, 1973.

Dreikurs, R. *Social Equality: The Challenge of Today.* Chicago: Contemporary Books, 1971.

———— and L. Grey. *A New Approach to Discipline: Logical Consequences.* New York: Hawthorn Books, 1968.

———— and V. Soltz. *Children: The Challenge.* New York: Hawthorn Books, 1964.

Ducette, J., S. Wolk, and E. Soucar. A typical pattern in locus of control and nonadaptive behavior. *Journal of Personality,* Vol. 40 (1972): 287–297.

Duncan, D. Attitudes towards parents and delinquency in suburban adolescent males. *Adolescence,* Vol. XII, No. 50 (Summary 1978): 365–369.

Forer, Lucille. *The Birth Order.* New York: McKay, 1976.

Frankel, J., and J. Dullaert. Is adolescent rebellion universal? *Adolescence,* Vol. XII, No. 46 (Summer 1977): 227–236.

Gabel, H. Effects of parental group discussion on adolescents' perceptions of maternal behavior. *Journal of Community Psychology,* Vol. 3, No. 1 (January 1975).

Glenn, H. Stephen. *Strengthening the Family.* Potomac Press. 1980.

Glenn, H. Stephen, and J. Warner. *Developing Capable Young People.* Hurst, Tex.: Humansphere, 1982.

Gordon, Thomas. *P.E.T.—Parent Effectiveness Training.* New York: Wyden, 1970.

Guzzetta, R. Acquisition and transfer of empathy by the parents of early adolescents through structured learning training *Journal of Counseling Psychology.* Vol. 23, No. 5 (1976): 449–453.

Harmin, Merill, Harold Kirschenbaum, and Sidney Simon. *Clarifying Values Through Subject Matter.* Minneapolis, Minn: Winston Press, 1973.

Herndon, James. *How to Survive in Your Native Land.* New York: Bantam, 1972.

Hetherington, E. Effects of father absence on personality development in adolescent daughters. *Developmental Psychology,* Vol. 7, No. 3 (1972).

Hoffman, M. Fathers' absence and conscience development. *Developmental Psychology,* Vol. 4, No. 3 (1971).

Jessor, S., and R. Jessor. Maternal ideology and adolescent problem behavior. *Developmental Psychology,* Vol. 10, No. 2 (1974): 246–254.

Kandel, D., R. Kessler, and R. Margulies. Antecedents of adolescent-initiation into stages of drug use: A developmental analysis. *Journal of Youth and Adolescence,* Vol. 7, No. 1 (1978): 13–48.

Kvols-Riedler, K., and B. Kvols-Riedler. *Redirecting Children's Misbehavior.* Boulder, Colo.: R.D.I.C. Publications, 1979.

Lawson, Gary, James Peterson, and Ann Lawson. *Alcoholism and the Family.* Rockville, Md.: An Aspen Publication, 1983.

Lesseigne, M. A study of peer and adult influence on moral benefits of adolescents. *Adolescence,* Vol. X, No. 38 (Summer 1975): 227–230.

Lockwood, A. The effects of values clarification and moral development criteria. *Review of Educational Research,* Vol. 48, No. 3 (Summer 1978): 325–364.

Lofquist, William *Understanding the Meaning of Prevention.* Youth Development Association, Phoenix, Ariz.: 1980.

Manet, Marsha. *Parents, Peers and Pot,* 2 vols. National Institute on Drug Abuse.

Marsella, A., R. Dubanoski, and K. Mohs. The effects of father presence and absence of maternal attitudes. *Journal of Genetic Psychology,* Vol. 125 (1974).

Nelsen, Jane. *Positive Discipline.* Fair Oaks, Calif.: Sunrise Press, 1981.

———. *Understanding.* Fair Oaks, Calif.: Sunrise Press, 1986.

Nihira, K., A. Usin, and R. Sinay. Perception of parental behavior by adolescents in crisis. *Psychological Reports,* Vol. 37 (1975): 787–793.

Norem-Hebeisen, A. A. Self-esteem as a predictor of adolescent drug abuse. In *Predicting Adolescent Drug Abuse* (1975), NIDA.

Nutt, Grady. *Family Time.* Des Plaines, Ill.: Million Dollar Round Table, 1977.

Plumb, M., C. D'Amanda, and Z. Taintor. Chemical substance abuse and perceived locus of control. In *Predicting Adolescent Drug Abuse* (1975), NIDA.

Robinson, P. Parents of beyond control adolescents. *Adolescence,* Vol. CIII, No. 49 (Spring 1978): 109–119.

Robinson, W. Boredom at school. *British Journal of Educational Psychology and Psychiatry,* Vol. 16 (1975).

Ryley, Helen, D. Dinkmeyer, E. Frierson, S. Glenn, and D. Shaw. *You've Got to be Kid-ding.* Boulder, Colo.: American Training Center, 1985.

Scheirer, M., and R. Kraut. Increasing educational achievement via self-concept change. *Review of Educational Research,* Vol. 49, No. 1 (Winter 1979): 131–150.

Simon, Sidney. *I Am Lovable and Capable.* Niles, Ill.: Argus Communications, 1973.

Small, Jacquelyn. *Becoming Naturally Therapeutic.* Austin, Tex.: Eupsychian Press, 1950.

Stanley, S. Family education to enhance the moral atmosphere of the family and the moral development of the adolescent. *Journal of Counseling Psychology,* Vol. 25, No. 2 (1978): 110–118.

Stinnett, N., and S. Taylor. Parent-child relationships and perceptions of alternate life styles. *Journal of Genetic Psychology* (1976): 129.

Stone, L., A. Miranne, and G. Ellis. Parent-peer influence as a predictor of marijuana use. *Adolescence,* Vol. XIV, No. 53 (Spring 1979): 115–122.

Streit, F. *EPAC Evaluation of Open Door Program* and *Evaluation of Project Redirection.* Highland Park, N.J.: Streit Associates, 1978.

———, Donald Halsted, and J. Pietro Pascale. Differences among youthful users and nonusers of drugs based on their perceptions of parental behavior. *International Journal of Addictions,* Vol. 9, No. 5 (1974): 749–755.

Tuckman, J., and R. Regan. Ordinal position and behavior problems in children. *Journal of Health and Social Behavior,* Vol. 12 (March 1971).

Valles, Jorges. *From Social Drinking to Alcoholism.* Dallas, Tex.: Tane Press, 1972.

Wadsworth, Bary J. *Piaget's Theory of Cognitive Development.* New York and London: Longmans, 1971.

Wolk, S., and J. Brandon. Runaway adolescents' perceptions of parents and self. *Adolescence,* Vol. XII, No. 46 (Summer 1977): 175–187.

INDEX

ABOUT THE AUTHORS

 **Jane Nelsen** is a popular lecturer and coauthor of the entire POSITIVE DISCIPLINE series. She also wrote *From Here to Serenity: Four Principles for Understanding Who You Really Are.* She has appeared on *Oprah* and *Sally Jesse Raphael* and was the featured parent expert on the "National Parent Quiz," hosted by Ben Vereen. Jane is the mother of seven children and the grandmother of seventeen.

 **H. Stephen Glenn** is the creator of Developing Capable People, a course that teaches skills for living and building strong relationships in homes, schools, and organizations. He is the author of *7 Strategies for Developing Capable Students* and the coauthor of many books, including *Positive Discipline in the Classroom.* Steve is the father of four children, stepfather of three, and grandfather of ten. He has also been a foster father of several young children.

FOR MORE INFORMATION

The authors are available for lectures, workshops, and seminars for parents, parent educators, therapists, psychologists, social workers, nurses, counselors, school administrators, teachers, and corporations. (Lectures can be tailored to fit your needs.)

Workshops include:

- Positive Discipline in the Classroom (a two-day workshop or a one-day inservice)
- Parenting Teens: They Still Need You, But in Different Ways
- Teaching Parenting the Positive Discipline Way (a two-day workshop)
- Developing Capable People (a three-day workshop)
- How to Think, Feel, and Act Like a New Person

Workshops, seminars, and facilitator training are scheduled throughout the United States each year. To find a location near you or to bring a workshop to your area, contact:

Jane Nelsen   H. Stephen Glenn
Empowering People   1-800-456-7770
P.O. Box 1926
Orem, UT 84059-1926
1-800-456-7770

View www.positivediscipline.com for featured articles, answers to parent and teacher questions, and workshop and research information.

A Proven Program That Helps Every Child Succeed

The number one goal of every parent and educator is to help children become successful adults. To achieve this goal children must learn self-discipline, responsibility, and judgment—the very same principles that help them become good students.

7 Strategies for Developing Capable Students can help you nourish the skills necessary for your child to become a capable adult. No parent or educator should be without this invaluable book!

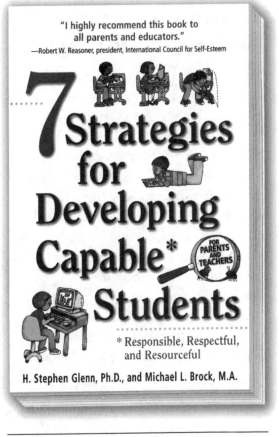

ISBN 0-7615-1356-6 / Paperback / 320 pages
U.S. $14.95 / Can. $22.95

THREE
RIVERS
PRESS

Available everywhere books are sold.
Visit us online at www.randomhouse.com.

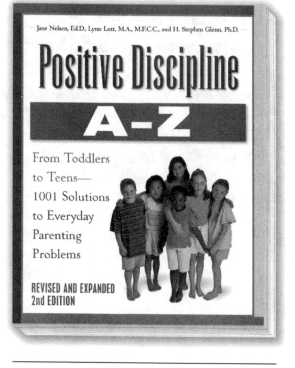